RAILROAD STATIONS

RAILROAD
STATIONS

BRIAN SOLOMON

CONTENTS

FOREWORD:
GRAND CENTRAL STATION........8

INTRODUCTION:
THE ROLE OF THE RAILROAD........12

CHAPTER 1:
DOWN AT THE DEPOT........26

CHAPTER 2:
UNION STATIONS........38

CHAPTER 3:
TERMINALS........48

CHAPTER 4:
CLASSIC STATIONS........74

CHAPTER 5:
GONE BUT NOT FORGOTTEN........96

CHAPTER 6:
ADAPTIVE REUSE........102

BIBLIOGRAPHY........116

INDEX........117

GRAND CENTRAL TERMINAL

I have been around railroad stations all my life, from tiny trackside shelters to the largest, busiest terminals. One of my early railroad station experiences was a trip to New York's Grand Central Terminal with my father when I was five. Toward the end of an overcast day, we boarded an electric Penn-Central commuter train several miles north of New York City on the Hudson Line. As we rode toward Grand Central, the lights of the city began to come on, punctuating the forbidding bleakness of the metropolis on a dull day. Our train paused at 125th Street Station in

Harlem, as do nearly all New York City–bound commuter runs, then proceeded the final four miles (6.5km) to the great station, running over the Park Avenue Viaduct and into the Park Avenue Tunnel. As we rolled into the station's lower level, I could see other trains headed outbound through the subterranean gloom. Our train came to rest gently at a bumping post. Unlike most of the passengers arriving at Grand Central that day, who had simply come to New York to work, to shop, or to visit friends, we had come to visit the world's greatest passenger station. We had come to see the station itself!

For many years, Grand Central was the largest and the busiest train station in the world. Its 103 tracks occupy two full levels below the streets of Manhattan. On both levels, loop tracks allow trains in the station to be reversed easily, though this feature is rarely used now. Loop tracks are found only at two major railway terminals in the world, Grand Central and South Station in Boston, although South Station never uses its underground loop. Grand Central Terminal is a vast city of interconnected underground passageways. The station's head house contains some of the most elegant features ever applied to a transport structure.

The present-day Grand Central Terminal replaced an earlier building, the Grand Central Depot. Built in the early 1870s, the depot had become overcrowded and congested. In 1904, under a mandate from the State legislature following a fatal collision in the smoke-filled approach tunnel, the New York Central began experimenting with electrification. By the time the new Grand Central was underway in 1906, all routes to the station were fully electrified, completely eliminating the use of polluting steam engines in Manhattan.

Grand Central Terminal was jointly designed by the Minnesota architectural firm of Reed & Stem and the local firm of Warren & Watmore; the result is a Beaux Arts architectural masterpiece. Grand Central's architects employed radical new designs to reduce congestion: the terminal has broad, gently sloping ramps instead of staircases to bring most passengers to their trains. The few stairs are very wide to minimize interruptions in the traffic flow. A lower-level concourse separating commuter from long-distance traffic vastly improved operating efficiency. Grand Central's builders anticipated continued growth of passenger traffic and designed the terminal to handle a greater volume of traffic than has ever existed; a second, lower-level, long-distance arrival station was built but never opened for passenger traffic. It is used today as a maintenance yard, completely invisible to the hordes of daily commuters who pass through the terminal. Unfortunately, shortly after Grand Central opened in 1913, the growth in passenger traffic began to level off as automobile travel gained popularity.

These facts eluded my young mind, but to me Grand Central was just about the most fascinating place imaginable. We explored the vast underground space, wandering briefly down one of the platforms to look at dual-powered, electric and diesel-electric FL9 locomotives specially designed for the New Haven Railroad's Grand Central operation by Electro Motive. We went into the lower-level concourse designed specifically for the needs of the hurried Manhattan commuter and my father demonstrated one of Grand Central's wonders, the Whispering Gallery, a four-cornered parabolic archway between the upper- and lower-level concourses. I stood in one corner and my father stood in the opposite corner many yards away. Through the science of acoustics, we could talk to one another in the faintest whispers, despite the noisy rush of passengers racing between us to catch the express to New Rochelle.

Upstairs we gazed at the constellations painted on the ceiling, gathered timetables from the rack at the gilded information booth in the center of the main concourse, and had a snack at the Oyster Bar, a Grand Central institution, opposite the Whispering Gallery. My dad had arranged to meet a friend there. This man worked for Penn-Central and would give us a tour of those areas of the station the public never sees.

First we took the elevators all the way to the top of the station, where there were rooms away from the bustle of daily passengers. We went to a glass-floored overlook hidden between the great windows along the sides of the main concourse and viewed the throngs of passengers far below, who looked like scurrying ants. Then we left the station and walked out into the streets of Manhattan. We walked along a side street until we reached an unmarked door on the side of the building. My father's friend unlocked the door and revealed a dark staircase dropping deep below ground. A waft of musty air greeted us as we descended the steel stairs that brought us to track level and into the very bowels of America's largest station. The stairs and connecting passage were dimly lit by incandescent bulbs. The roar of passing trains echoed throughout the tunnels. After a bit of a walk along a narrow catwalk, we ascended a short flight of stairs into one of Grand Central's switch towers—the station's nerve center, where the trains are routed onto their respective tracks.

It was not much brighter in the tower than it was in the tunnels. The tower operator greeted us, and in short order he explained the operation of the tower. A very long row of levers controlled the track switches and signals. I was coached in their operation and was soon assisting the operator in his duties. This was an interlocking tower, meaning that the levers, switches, and signals were all mechanically interlocked to prevent trains from being lined into one another. It was fail-safe, and even a carefully directed five-year-old could set switches without the risk of accident. The worst that could happen if a signal was not set properly was a minor delay to an incoming train.

The visit was all too brief. Before I knew it, we were riding out of Grand Central past the tower I had just been in, and back the way we had come. I knew I would return to Grand Central again!

Brian Solomon, 1997

PAGE 8: *The design for New York's Grand Central Terminal was changed several times before the final form was settled on. Today the station's façade is one of the best known in the city. The statuary around the clock is the work of sculptor Jules Coutan.* PAGE 9: *Grand Central Terminal was designed to efficiently separate local commuters from long-distance passengers. The station currently only serves commuters using Metro North, the commuter line that runs north of New York City; all long-distance trains to the city now use Penn Station.* OPPOSITE: *Grand Central Terminal's main concourse is a magnificent, awe-inspiring space—the ceiling rises 125 feet (37.5m) above the floor. While one of the most memorable parts of the great station, the concourse is only one portion of the historic terminal.*

THE ROLE OF THE RAILROAD

Railways were first developed in the 1820s in Britain. George Stephenson and others perfected the reciprocating steam locomotive and adapted it to railway use. The advantages of railroad transportation over canals and horse-drawn wagons were astounding. A trip that had taken all day now only required a few hours; long overland journeys that had required weeks took only a few days. Railroad fever gripped the Western nations, and from the mid-1830s until after the turn of the century, thousands of miles of railroad were constructed every year.

During this period a new type of building sprung up in cities and towns everywhere, a structure specifically designed for railway passengers, where they could wait in comfort and board trains in all sorts of weather—the railroad depot. Before the advent of the railway, no comparable structure had ever existed on such a large scale. Often the depot was the most important and most attractive building in a community. Tens of thousands of railroad stations were built around the world. The greatest number and the greatest variety of railroad depots were built in the United States.

CHANGES IN RAILWAY TRAVEL IN THE TWENTIETH CENTURY

After World War I, railway travel in Europe and the United States followed radically different paths. Most European nations nationalized their railways and made a concerted effort to maintain and improve railroad passenger service. While the level and nature of improvement have varied considerably from nation to nation, in general, main lines were electrified and train speeds were increased to compete with the automobile. In 1981, super-high-speed TGV (Très Grande Vitesse) trains running at 150 mph to 185 mph (241.5kph to 297.5kph) were introduced in France, demonstrating how rail travel could compete with short-haul air travel and be profitable as well. Super-high-speed rail service is being introduced all over Europe.

European railways are well integrated with one another and with other transportation modes. In Amsterdam, Frankfort, Geneva, and Zurich, main-line corridor trains stop directly under airport terminals.

The Netherlands features a splendid railway network. Immaculate electric trains stop at every major town and village on relatively frequent schedules. As is typical in Europe, most Dutch trains feature both first- and second-class cars, allowing passengers who wish to pay a slightly higher fare the opportunity to travel in greater comfort.

Like many European nations, the Netherlands was devastated in World War II, and afterward much of its railway network was entirely rebuilt. New, modern structures replaced many of the classic stations that had been destroyed. The stations at Eindhoven and Breda are examples of efficient but spartan-looking depots. The main station in Amsterdam is one of the few great Dutch stations to survive the war. Its nineteenth-century multiple-span arched train shed and traditional waiting room host hundreds of trains and passengers daily.

DECLINE OF RAIL TRAVEL IN THE UNITED STATES

In the United States, passenger rail traffic suffered a long, slow decline after World War I, and today many Americans are unaware that their country once had a truly great network of passenger rail lines. Virtually every city and town in the country had at least one railroad depot, and passenger trains operated everywhere from Van Buren, Maine, to Washington State's Olympic Peninsula, and from the Florida Keys to the Southern California deserts. In the Midwest, crack passenger trains, which were fast long-distance trains which railroad companies named, regularly operated at more than one hundred miles per hour (161kph). The Milwaukee Road ran the *Hiawathas* between Chicago and Milwaukee at 105 mph (169kph) in the 1930s, using conventional, reciprocating steam locomotives. No fancy turbo-powered, tilting, articulated trains or government subsidies were needed.

However fast or comfortable select passenger trains in the United States once were, they were forsaken by the public in favor of automobile and airplane travel. By the early 1970s, passenger service had reached an all-time low. In 1971, Congress relieved the railroads of their growing long-distance passenger deficit by creating Amtrak to maintain a bare minimum of intercity rail service. Within the next fifteen years, most remaining commuter operations came under various state agencies, so that by the mid-1980s the traditional railroad companies were strictly freight haulers with virtually all passenger service under some public control or ownership. Rail travel in Canada followed a similar pattern, although several small, privately owned railroads continue to operate passenger trains. During this long decline, many railroad stations were destroyed, relocated, or converted to other uses, such as maintenance depots, offices, or freight agencies, or were sold to private individuals.

Since the early 1980s, United States rail travel, particularly commuter operations in large cities, has undergone a limited renaissance, usually with federal or state aid. Some states, such as California, subsidize long-distance trains as well. However, the primary long-distance carrier, Amtrak, is perpetually on the edge of oblivion, as its federal funding remains continually subject to partisan scrutiny and budget trimming. Only in the heavily traveled Northeast Corridor between Boston, Massachusetts, and Washington, D.C., has there been any real advance toward the sort of high-speed rail service now common in most of Europe and Japan.

PAGE 12: *The monumental station at Milan, Italy, was one of the last great classical railway stations built in Europe. One if its arched sheds spans 310 feet (94.5m) —among the largest ever built.* PAGE 13: *The modern Part Dieu railway station in Lyons, France, was designed by architect Santiago Calatrava. It was built to serve the high-speed Très Grande Vitesse trains.* OPPOSITE: *European station designers tried to match a depot's architecture with the city it was intended to serve. The colorfully decorated Karlsplatz station in Vienna, Austria, was designed by Otto Wagner and completed about 1900. While most railroad stations in the United States were privately owned until the 1970s, European railways had been nationalized by World War II and the depots were viewed as public works.*

London's Victoria Station was originally two separate stations side by side. The older of the two stations, seen here, is the Central Side, built in 1860. The other station, known as the Chatham Side, was built in 1862. The facilities were integrated in the 1920s, and today Victoria hosts up to 200,000 passengers a day.

PAGES 18-19: *Tokyo's Shin-Juku station is reported to be the busiest in the world. Hundreds of trains serve this facility every day. Unlike most traditional railroad stations, Shin-Juku does not have distinctive architecture; instead the station facilities are blended with the surrounding shopping plazas and department stores.* LEFT: *Architect Marius Toudoire made prolific use of the arch in his Gare de Lyon in Paris. The exterior of the station is known for its oversized clock tower.* ABOVE: *The vast arched train sheds at Milan were completed a generation after that style of construction had fallen out of favor elsewhere in the world. Few arched sheds were built after the introduction of the Bush shed in 1904.*

ABOVE: *When it was built, Louis de la Censerie's Central Station in Antwerp, Belgium, was considered a transitional station design between a traditional and a more modern style. It was completed around the turn of the century, survived World War II, and still serves as it was intended then.* RIGHT: *The station of Frankfort on the Main is one of the most impressive in Europe, if for no other reason than its sheer size—it is the largest in Germany. The train shed alone spans 549 feet (167.3m). The station and shed took nearly a decade to build.*

OPPOSITE, RIGHT, AND BELOW: *The French Très Grande Vitesse (TGV) high-speed trains use a new, specially graded line that was built specifically for them. Many new stations were built for the TGV, including this one at Lyons, built about 1980. While rail service in the United States was allowed to deteriorate gradually, the Europeans made a considerable investment in their lines, as shown by this station.*

CHAPTER 1

DOWN AT THE DEPOT

In the days before the advent of the automobile and telephone, the railroad station was the principal transportation and communications center in town, and often a social center, too. Train time was the most important time of the day; it was not unusual for everyone in town to know the passenger train schedules by heart. Since railroads used the telegraph to dispatch trains, the station was also the telegraph office. As a result, the station agent or operator had the best connections with the outside world and was the first to get important news and information.

PAGE 26: *The depot at Laurel, Maryland, was one of many stations designed for the Baltimore & Ohio by E. Francis Baldwin. Baldwin also designed B&O's Oakland and Mt. Royal, Maryland, stations, opposite and pictured on pages 114–115. Many depots in Pennsylvania and Maryland are made of bricks, a building material produced locally.* PAGE 27: *At Woodsville, New Hampshire, this three-story wooden station once hosted passenger trains of the Boston & Maine Railroad. Boston & Maine lines used to blanket much of New Hampshire and Massachusetts, but today many have been abandoned. The depot is now used by a variety of shops.* ABOVE: *One of Chicago's finest stations was North Western Passenger Station, designed by Charles S. Frost and Alfred Hoyt Granger. It was built between 1906 and 1911 and demolished in the mid-1980s. Its replacement is a modern "glass box" that also serves as an office building.*

The railroad station was the first place visitors would see, so there was considerable civic pride in the depot's appearance. Each community wanted a distinctive building, since its size and style reflected the town's status in relation to its neighbor's. A larger town usually warranted a larger and more attractive station than a small town. Frequently towns built parks and gardens around their railroad stations, and railroads hosted garden competitions along the line to beautify the area.

The golden age of station building in the United States and Canada began about 1870, ending shortly after the turn of the century. During this time an estimated fifteen thousand to thirty thousand passenger stations were built in the United States, and roughly another five thousand stations were built in Canada.

Railroad stations had to withstand heavy use for a long period of time and were generally built to higher standards than residences and shops. Stations were built to standard plans that incorporated a waiting room, a baggage area, an agent's office, and platforms. This dictated a building's layout and dimensions but not necessarily its style. Few other buildings with a common purpose and similar designs have displayed a greater variety of architectural styles than railroad stations, which varied greatly from railroad to railroad, from community to community, and from region to region.

The architectural style of a depot often reflected local preferences and available materials. Originally, most depots were simple wooden structures, but as the railroads prospered these were often replaced with more elaborate

stations. Many New England stations were constructed of local granite; Midwestern depots were often built from limestone; in Pennsylvania and Maryland, red brick was preferred; and in the West, stucco, terra cotta, and tile were often used.

In the northeastern United States, particularly in New England, Gothic Revival, Federalist, Colonial Revival, and Romanesque styles were popular, while in the American Southwest—and also in Florida—the Spanish Mission style was favored. In England, many depots were built in a Tudor style. Railroads had their favorite architects. The Baltimore & Ohio employed E. Francis Baldwin, who designed dozens of Baltimore & Ohio stations, from small country depots to colorful resort stations like the Queen Anne–style brick

The town of Oakland, Maryland, along the Baltimore & Ohio, was awarded a better-than-average depot because it was a popular mountain resort area. In the mid-1880s, B&O's architect, E. Francis Baldwin, designed this Queen Anne–style brick station, which features a distinctive rounded tower and handsome slate roof.

OPPOSITE: *The Santa Fe railroad station at Barstow, California, included a Harvey House restaurant, as did many of the railroad's larger stations. It was designed by Francis W. Wilson, who melded elements from Spanish and Moroccan architectural styles.* ABOVE: *Many small-town depots were relatively utilitarian affairs, yet solidly built and readily identifiable as railroad stations. The small former Denver Rio Grande & Western station at Thompson, Utah, still serves Amtrak as a "flag stop," a station where passenger trains will stop only on signal.*

building in Oakland, Maryland. The Boston & Albany hired Henry Hobson Richardson, one of America's foremost nineteenth-century architects. The Chicago & North Western preferred the work of Charles S. Frost (see sidebar, page 36).

Most stations had at least one full-time employee, commonly an agent/operator who was responsible for day-to-day operations: assisting passengers with travel plans, selling tickets, taking care of baggage, and monitoring the telegraph. Orders, written in specific language as directed by rule books, would come over telegraph wires for trains passing through stations. These orders would either supplement or supplant the timetable, authorizing trains to occupy the tracks or pass one another in a synchronized and safe manner. The agent/operator was responsible for translating the orders from Morse code and delivering them to passing trains. This was

often done by raising a train order signal at the station and then handing up the orders hooked to a wire on a long pole to the train crew as the train passed by. This process was called handing up orders on the fly. The railroad station also served as a principal mail drop for small towns. Passenger trains carried Railway Post Office cars, where mail was sorted en route, and mailbags were picked up and dropped off on the fly as the train sped through town. Special equipment was used to position mailbags from the depot to be grabbed by the train crew, and hooks were set up to snag the mailbags from the train as the Railway Post Office cars passed. In many rural areas, the station agent lived at the depot with his family. Larger depots employed several people, including a station agent, operator, baggage handler, and express agent.

In the days before dining cars, railroads provided eating stops on long runs. Trains would pause at a station, and passengers would have ten minutes to half an hour to eat before boarding again. Fred Harvey, a British-born entrepreneur, made his fortune by operating quality railroad restaurants along the Santa Fe line. In his travels, he had found the railroad dining experience intolerable and saw opportunity in making it more pleasant. He served only the best food and hired attractive young women to serve his customers. By the turn of the century, there were Harvey House restaurants at depots all along the Santa Fe line, from Illinois to California.

While many depots survive, their premier role in the community waned long ago. The small-town railroad station is now a relic of another, long-ago age.

ELLICOTT CITY
America's Oldest Depot

Nestled in the rustic Patapsco River Valley, only a few miles from Baltimore, Maryland, is Ellicott City, a classic early American town that is home to America's oldest still-standing train station. The Baltimore & Ohio Railroad, the nation's first common-carrier rail line, was chartered to build tracks between Baltimore and the Ohio River in 1827, and by 1830 it had reached Ellicott's Mills, now Ellicott City, thirteen miles (21km) west of Baltimore. Ellicott's Mills was an established manufacturing center, and here the Baltimore & Ohio met the Frederick Turnpike, the principal east–west highway in the area. To serve this important town, the railroad built a solid freight station of wood and stone. Although this building seems small today, it was quite large by contemporary standards. Originally, passengers did not use this depot; instead they purchased their tickets and boarded trains at a nearby hotel, which is also still standing.

The Baltimore & Ohio began operating before there were practical steam locomotives in the United States, so initially it used horses to pull its primitive trains. This arrangement lasted only a few years. By 1832, the railroad had acquired several early, vertical-boiler, grasshopper-type locomotives and needed a place to house them in Ellicott's Mills. It expanded its freight station by adding a two-stall engine house, and eventually the railroad moved its passenger facilities into the station as well.

To accommodate the geographical constraints of the narrow, winding Patapsco Valley, the Baltimore & Ohio arrived in Ellicott's Mills at a higher level than the main street of the town. Traveling west over the Oliver Viaduct, it crossed both the Frederick Turnpike and Tiber Creek in downtown, and then hugged a narrow shelf, which continued westward along the Patapsco River. The route necessitated the building of the depot on two levels, putting the historic structure in character with the rest of the town. The top level was even with the tracks and, in later years, contained a small ticket office,

The agent's office at Ellicott City is a typical setting for a nineteenth-century ticket agent. As its name suggests, Relay, Maryland—once an important station located just a few miles east of Ellicott City—was where teams of horses were exchanged before the Baltimore & Ohio used steam locomotives, Later, the Ellicott City depot was one of the B&O's first enginehouses.

waiting room, and baggage-handling area in addition to the engine house. The lower level held living quarters for the station agent and his family. These were the typical elements of small railroad stations throughout the United States and Canada. Except for its unorthodox, two-level arrangement, the Ellicott's Mills depot was in many ways a prototype for the tens of thousands of small-town American train stations that followed it.

Changes in American transport affected Ellicott City just after World War II. Passenger trains stopped serving the town in 1949, and in 1973 the railroad stopped using the station altogether. However, it had been placed on the National Register of Historic Places in 1968, and after its useful life as a railroad structure came to an end, it was converted into a museum. In November 1996, CSX Transportation, the successor to the old Baltimore & Ohio, conveyed ownership of the historic structure to the local government. The railroad and museum conducted a ceremony in which a replica of Peter Cooper's Tom Thumb—the first American-built locomotive—chugged triumphantly into the station, thus recreating the mythic event of more than 160 years earlier. Today the depot is home to the Ellicott City Baltimore & Ohio Railroad Museum, which is undertaking a historical restoration of the ancient building. Meanwhile the tracks in front of the station still host a half dozen heavy freight trains daily.

A replica of Peter Cooper's locomotive, the first American-built steam locomotive to haul a train, poses in front of the Ellicott City station. In 1830 Peter Cooper demonstrated his locomotive to the Baltimore & Ohio by running it from Baltimore to Ellicott's Mills, today Ellicott City.

CHAPTER 2

UNION STATIONS

I n the heyday of the railroad, it was not unusual to find two or more

railroad companies serving the same small town. Most large cities had

at least two lines. At first, every railroad had its own depot, and it

was rare for railroads to share facilities. However, as railroads grew it

became desirable to build combined—or union—stations at key locations,

with benefits for all the parties involved. Separate stations presented difficul-

ties if passengers had to transfer from one line to another. A union station

made traveling easier for both the through passenger and the local passenger

by centralizing facilities and making connections simpler. The community also benefited because union stations usually permitted the railroads to invest in more glamorous, larger depots than they would have built separately. Most important to the railroads, by pooling resources they could reduce operating costs and, perhaps, increase patronage.

JOLIET UNION STATION

Joliet, Illinois, located just west of Chicago, was crossed by several railroads. By the turn of the century, the volume of traffic moving to and from Chicago—the nation's busiest railroad interchange—was enormous, and Joliet's streets were continually blocked by trains. In 1906, the city demanded grade separation (raising the tracks above the street to relieve traffic congestion and improve safety) of the three busiest

PAGE 38: *The majesty of Chicago Union Station is a remnant of the great years of American rail service. The sign in the main waiting room directs passengers to the concourse where one can still board trains for New York City, Boston, New Orleans, Los Angeles, Denver, Seattle, and Toronto.*

PAGE 39: *St. Louis Union Station once served many railroads, including New York Central, Pennsylvania, Gulf Mobile & Ohio, and Missouri Pacific. When it was built, its architects won a design competition for its exquisite style. Today it has been adapted to non-railroad use.*

RIGHT: *Joliet Union Station, designed by noted railroad station architect Jarvis Hunt, is noteworthy for its unusual hexagonal shape. It was built in conjunction with an elaborate project to elevate the railroad tracks in Joliet, since heavy railroad traffic had made street travel difficult. The city bought interest in the station in the 1980s and restored the decaying building; it was rededicated in 1991.*

railroads in town: Rock Island, Chicago & Alton, and Santa Fe. In conjunction with this project, Joliet Union Station was built at the junction of the three lines. It was designed by noted railroad architect Jarvis Hunt, who is also responsible for Kansas City's Union Station and Southern Pacific's Sixteenth Street Station in Oakland, California. Hence, these three stations bear a strong family resemblance.

Joliet Union features a classic Beaux Arts design. The unique hexagon structure—a function of the unusual angle at which the tracks meet the station—is built of beige limestone from Bedford, Indiana. The waiting room has a forty-five-foot-high (13.5m) vaulted ceiling and large arched windows. Ornate bronze fixtures decorate the station inside and out, and large hanging bronze canopies shelter the platform entrances to the station. Passengers enter the station from street level and board trains on the second level.

When Joliet Union station was first built, it was served by both city streetcars and interurban electric trains at street level, in addition to passenger trains from the three steam railroads on the second level. Joliet developed into a convenient suburban stop for many long-distance trains headed for Chicago. Santa Fe's Chief, San Francisco Chief, and Grand Canyon Limited all paused here, as did Rock Island's famous Rocky Mountain Rocket and the Alton Route's Midnight Special. Rock Island's heavily patronized commuter trains from Chicago's La Salle Street Station terminated here.

In the 1960s and 1970s, Joliet Union declined, many of the famous train routes were discontinued, and the station fell into disrepair. The station was acquired by the city in the mid-1980s and was restored and rededicated in 1991. Today it still functions as a union station, serving dozens of Chicago-area Metra commuter trains and a half dozen long-distance Amtrak trains a day.

LEFT: *The Rio Grande Ski Train lays over at Denver Union Station. This fine building once served passenger trains of the Rio Grande, Union Pacific, Burlington, Rock Island, and Santa Fe railroad lines. The neon sign encourages the public to "travel by train," a message often ignored in the jet age.*

DENVER UNION STATION

Several blocks west of downtown Denver, Colorado, lies Denver Union Station, an impressive Beaux Arts–inspired, Neoclassical, steel-framed granite building featuring a large red neon sign reading "Travel by Train." The station, which was designed by architects Taylor, Van Brundt and Howe, has an unusual history. The present structure, completed in 1914, was built from the ruins of an earlier station of Romanesque design that was mostly destroyed by fire. It is one of the few large American railroad stations that once served both standard-gauge and narrow-gauge trains. Denver Union also served interurban electric trains for several decades. The platforms are reached from the waiting room by a network of well-lit subterranean passageways to avoid having passengers cross the railroad tracks. A large welcome arch once stood in front of the station facing Seventeenth Street but, in 1931, in a victory of function over beauty, the decorative arch was deemed a traffic hazard and removed.

In its heyday, Denver Union employed six hundred people and served some eighty daily trains. By the early 1950s, Denver Union Station was in decline, serving only forty or so daily trains. Gradually all the great trains were discontinued. Even the fabulous California Zephyr was dropped, in 1970. Throughout the 1970s and into the early 1980s, Denver Union remained the eastern terminus of the Rio Grande Zephyr, the last remainder of the California Zephyr. For several years in the early 1980s, amid a sea of Amtrak monotony, the Rio Grande Zephyr had the distinction of being the last regularly scheduled, privately operated, long-distance passenger train in the United States. Eventually, even this distinctive passenger train came under the operation of Amtrak.

Today, the area around Denver Union at Seventeenth and Wynkoop streets is a popular, revitalized neighborhood of the Mile High City. Surrounded by shops and trendy restaurants, the station retains much of its former glory, although the great chandeliers and candelabras that once illuminated the interior have been removed. The second and third floors of the grand building serve as offices, albeit in most cases for companies other than the railroads. The waiting room and ticket areas serve the purpose for which they were intended, and the station still looks like a true railroad station,

unlike many of its modern counterparts, which resemble airport and bus terminals. Denver Union still features a traditional railroad lunch counter and large wooden benches.

CHICAGO UNION STATION

Although Chicago has never enjoyed a single unified terminal, it has had a Union Station of one sort or another for nearly 140 years. The first Chicago Union Station was built in 1858 and destroyed by the Great Chicago Fire of 1871. The second Union Station, constructed by Pennsylvania Railroad's Chicago-area predecessor, Pittsburgh, Fort Wayne & Chicago, was completed in 1880. This handsome Victorian station was constructed mostly of brick, with stone trim for its arched windows and doorways. Iron cantilevered canopies surrounded the front of the building. In addition to the Fort Wayne Line, it was served by the Milwaukee Road, the Burlington, and the Chicago & Alton (a predecessor of the Gulf, Mobile & Ohio, a railroad that merged in the 1970s with the Illinois Central).

Chicago's strategic location on Lake Michigan and as a principal east–west railroad junction fueled enormous growth in railroad use following the Great Fire of 1871. By 1912, on the eve of World War I, Chicago Union Station had become cramped and outmoded. In 1913, the three principal users of Union Station—the Pennsylvania Railroad, Burlington, and Milwaukee Road—formed a Chicago Union Station Company to build and operate a new station. Work on the new station began in 1914 but was interrupted by the war and not completed until 1925. The original plan for the new station was executed by Daniel Burnham, who also designed Washington Union Station, but he died before the station was completed. The design was revised by the firm Graham, Anderson, Probst & White, a firm that also worked on the Cleveland Union Terminal and Pennsylvania Railroad's Philadelphia Thirtieth Street Station. Chicago Union was among the last of the large American stations to employ a Beaux Arts design and a classical motif.

Chicago Union is essentially two stub-end terminals back to back. The south end, which features fourteen tracks, hosted trains of the Burlington, Pennsylvania, and tenant Gulf, Mobile & Ohio, while the north end has just

ten tracks and served only trains of the Milwaukee Road. Two tracks run between the two stub ends, allowing trains to run through, north to south. The station itself was divided into two principal parts: the main waiting room and the concourse, connected by an underground passageway. The entrance to the station is at street level, and the tracks are in a trench below the street. A U-shaped driveway brings traffic into the station building from the city streets by way of long ramps into the concourse area to speed the pickup of passengers. The exterior is constructed from Indiana limestone, and with its rows of massive Tuscan columns, resembled New York's Pennsylvania Station.

In 1969, Chicago Union's passenger concourse was demolished to make way for an office building. A new concourse of little architectural merit was incorporated in the office structure. The main waiting room with its large overhead skylights and tall columns was preserved and restored. Today it is the last active remnant of the many fine railroad stations that once served the Chicago area.

LEFT: *The union station at Palmer, Massachusetts, was designed by noted American architect H.H. Richardson for the Boston & Albany Railroad. Richardson and his successors—Shepley, Rutan & Coolidge—designed many stations for the B&A. This one also served the New London Northern, later the Central Vermont Railway, which crossed the B&A at Palmer.*

ABOVE: *Chicago Union Station's exterior as it appeared in the 1940s. A portion of the station was torn down in the late 1960s to make room for an office complex, while the main waiting room remains in daily use.* OPPOSITE: *Chicago Union Station's main waiting room as seen today. This is the last of the great Chicago stations still in use, and it still functions as a union station—thousands of Amtrak and Metra passengers change trains here everyday.*

CHAPTER 3

TERMINALS

In the railroad's heyday, the largest, busiest, and most impressive railway stations were big-city terminals, a railroad's crown jewels. Terminals featured distinctive architecture and were designed by well-known, greatly esteemed architects. They were among a city's most imposing edifices, ranking with cathedrals, royal palaces, and capitol buildings. Before airline and automobile travel, the railway terminal was the principal inland gateway to a city and was treated with great respect.

PAGE 48: *The Gare de Lyon in Paris was the work of architect Marius Toudoire, while its train shed was executed by engineer M. Denis. This station, completed in 1900, is only two miles from the Gare d'Orsay, built at about the same time.* PAGE 49: *Cologne's terminal was built in the 1890s, when "shed-only" stations were popular in Germany. Though this is a through station and has a full set of approach tracks at both ends, it is also a terminal—many trains begin and end their journeys here. Beyond the station is the Dom, a medieval Gothic cathedral, one of Germany's best-known buildings.* OPPOSITE: *Despite its distinctly Moorish appearance, the railway terminal at Kuala Lumpur, Malaysia, was built by the British in 1911. This station clearly demonstrates the two principal components of many large railway terminals: the station building (left) and the train shed (right).* ABOVE: *The arched train shed in Cologne, Germany, is one of the longest ever built and one of many such "balloon"-style sheds still in use in Europe. Visiting Americans are often awed by the vastness of the shed and impressed by the quality and frequency of German trains.*

Big terminals were intended to handle a large and often increasing volume of passenger traffic, so they had to be designed for efficiency. Aesthetically, they were designed to inspire awe and confidence and to encourage railway travel. Terminal buildings were among the most significant architectural accomplishments of the nineteenth century, and some remain as examples of the finest architecture in the world.

TRAIN SHEDS

The two principal components of most terminals are the station and the boarding area. During the first hundred years of terminal design, sheds of several types were used to shelter passengers from the elements as they boarded trains. The largest, most elaborate sheds could usually be found at the biggest terminals and, not surprisingly, where the weather is the worst: in the United Kingdom, Northern Europe, and the northeastern and midwestern United States. Early sheds were little more than glorified barns. By the late 1830s, iron sheds came into use in England. But the best known are large, single-span, arched, iron and glass balloon-type train sheds inspired by London's Crystal Palace, which was erected in 1850. These big train sheds were constructed in the United States and Europe during a forty-year period, beginning in 1863 with St. Pancras

Station in London. The arched shed was the nineteenth century's most significant architectural innovation; it transcended the traditional definition of wall and ceiling and perfectly combined beauty with functionality. The 240-foot-wide (73m), 100-foot-high (30.5m) St. Pancras arch, the work of William Henry Barlow, was the prototype for dozens of similar sheds constructed around the world. Cornelius Vanderbilt's first Grand Central Station in New York, which was built between 1869 and 1871, took its inspiration from St. Pancras. Not only did Grand Central feature a large, arched iron shed, it also boasted an elaborate, ornate head house. Grand Central Station is considered by many to be the first architecturally significant

Deco style with pastel interior decoration. The station's head house incorporates a tremendous arch resembling a gigantic tabletop radio of the period. In many respects, Cincinnati Union Terminal was the epitome of modern railroad station architecture in the United States.

Only a few large terminal projects were undertaken in the United States during the Great Depression. In 1933, at Thirtieth Street in Philadelphia, the Pennsylvania Railroad opened an impressive new through station, which mixed Neoclassical colonnaded entrances with Art Deco motifs. The last large terminal built in the United States was Los Angeles Union Passenger Terminal, completed in 1939. LAUPT served trains on the Union Pacific, Southern Pacific, and Santa Fe railroads. Major station building in Canada continued for a few more years. Montreal's Central Station (Gare Centrale), which is below street level on all but its southern extremity, was substantially completed during World War II. But construction on connected office buildings, shopping plazas, and its main hotel, La Reine Elisabeth, continued into the 1950s and 1960s.

In the United States, as passenger traffic tapered off in the 1920s, existing facilities proved more than capable of handling the reduced levels of traffic. Some newer terminals that were designed to handle an increasing ridership never reached their full capacity. In the United States and Canada, the volume of rail passengers dropped precipitously, leaving once-great terminals nearly without trains. Railroads were not always able to justify the expense of operating large terminals, and beginning in the 1950s, but especially after the federal government took over passenger service with Amtrak in 1971, many terminals were abandoned in favor of smaller, spartan, and less costly facilities. On the Continent, where almost all railroads have been owned by their national governments since World War I, passenger services have been heavily subsidized. As a result, major passenger terminals that survived World War II have been maintained and improved, and city stations are still well patronized.

LEFT: *In recent years Waterloo Station has come to host the distinctive-looking Eurostar trains, which carry passengers through the "Chunnel"—the long tunnel beneath the English Channel—to France and Belgium.*

In Britain, the situation is mixed. Luckily, only a few stations were destroyed in the bombing raids of World War II, and in the main cities, especially London, heavy commuter service has kept most of the nineteenth-century behemoths intact. But severe urban deterioration in some cities, and urban renewal or architectural modernization in others, have destroyed some venerable landmarks, including London's Euston and Broad Street stations. On the other hand, architectural preservationists have restored magnificent examples of Victorian railroad architecture such as London's Liverpool Street and St. Pancras terminals.

STUB-END VERSUS THROUGH STATIONS

The most prevalent type of terminal is the stub-end head-type. Stub-end tracks come in to the station from one direction and stop. Through trains must back out of the station, after making a stop, to rejoin the main line, a move that is costly and time-consuming. North and South stations in Boston, Dearborn Street and Chicago & North Western in Chicago, Grand Central in New York, and most of the great terminals in London and Paris are stub-end, head-type terminals. This type was favored in the early days of railroading and, despite its operational inflexibility, it remains popular in many cities worldwide. In large cities, stub-end terminals have several advantages over through stations. When the majority of passengers on incoming trains are destined for the city itself, a head-type station can be more cost-effective. Property in cities is at a premium, and head-type stations require far less real estate than through terminals, whose networks of tracks, interlocking connections, and crossings must be duplicated on both sides of the station. Another advantage to stub-end stations is that platform access is simpler. Passengers can proceed directly from the head house to the platforms, while multiple-platform through stations require elaborate, space-consuming concourses above or below track level with ramps and stairways.

However, as railroad lines developed into complex systems, through stations, in which tracks come into the station from two or more directions, gained popularity. With stub-end terminals, continuous train service cannot be accomplished without continually reversing train direction and sometimes changing engines, a practice still found in numerous European operations. In the United States prior to the turn of the century large through stations were relatively rare, but they became more common in the twentieth century. When the Pennsylvania Railroad—the largest passenger carrier in the United States during the first two-thirds of this century—modernized its plant, it phased out its major stub-end terminals in Jersey City and Philadelphia. Today, former Pennsylvania Railroad stations in New York City, Newark, Philadelphia (Thirtieth Street), Baltimore, and Harrisburg are among the busiest through stations in the nation. In Canada, Toronto Union Station is a heavily used multitrack through station, as is Central Station in Montreal, which is mostly used for commuter services. Through stations are popular in some European countries, particularly the Netherlands, Germany, and Belgium. Large through main stations are part of a continuous urban rail distribution route in Continental cities, including Amsterdam, Rotterdam, Cologne, Berlin, Hamburg, Copenhagen, Stockholm, Madrid, and Brussels. In Japan, stub-end terminals are rare except at the far ends of a line, and almost all the former Japanese National Railway stations are through or part of a loop, as in Tokyo and Osaka. However, much of the extensive private railways in Japan, which run like the electric interurbans did in North America some seventy years ago, are mostly stub-end in the big cities, since they tend to serve just two or three points as commuter lines.

PASSENGERS

At most passenger facilities, railroads must cater to two entirely different breeds of travelers, each with distinctive needs: daily commuters and long-distance travelers. Railroads shaped the growth of cities by changing the way people moved in their daily lives and creating suburbia. Before the railroad, nearly everyone walked to work, but railroads allowed people to live many miles from their places of employment. Commuting by train was a late-nineteenth-century and early-twentieth-century phenomenon that first appeared in large American and European cities. Initially the railroads were not interested in commuter traffic. British railways in particular preferred to carry only the upper classes and were reluctant to encourage the masses to use trains. Indeed, the early British trains had four classes of service, with the lower two being hardly more than open carts on wheels with wooden slats to sit

on. Eventually, railroads realized that commuter traffic could be very lucrative, especially since it helped develop real estate along their lines, and the railroads began marketing and designing their routes, stations, and terminals accordingly. The term "commute" derives from the railroads' policy to reduce, or commute, their normal fares for frequent daily travelers.

In many ways, railroad commuters are ideal passengers. Their needs are very simple: they wish to travel as expeditiously, safely, and economically as possible. They require minimal frills, often purchase their tickets in advance, frequently ride the same train everyday, and, except for a briefcase and a newspaper, they carry no luggage. Commuter trains use the least complicated equipment, and their passengers do not require luxurious waiting rooms, parlors, or elaborate services. Commuter trains do not require a complex mix of car types and usually operate in a straightforward way. However, commuters wish to arrive and depart all at the same terminal simultaneously. This can lead to extreme congestion and terrible inefficiency, and railroads must build large terminal facilities that will be used to full capacity for only a few hours each day.

Long-distance passengers demand an entirely different set of logistics than do daily commuters. Speed and safety are important, but long-distance passengers require more elaborate trains than commuters. They have more involved terminal needs as well, requiring large waiting rooms, baggage facilities and porters, ticket counters, lunchrooms, and so on. Long-distance trains involve not just coaches but sleeping cars, baggage cars, mail cars, and observation cars, and they need more attention at the terminal than simple commuter trains. Staging yards and switch engines are needed to assemble the long-distance trains, and the order is important; the observation car has to be on the end of the train and the mail up front.

While commuters largely travel singly, long-distance travelers tend to travel in groups; they may be families with children unaccustomed to travel and easily disoriented. Whereas the commuter knows the schedule by rote, the long-distance passenger does not even know what platform the train leaves from. The commuter will march into the station two minutes before departure, while long-distance passengers will arrive two hours early. Commuters mainly want to travel inbound in the morning and outbound in the afternoon, but long-distance travelers come and go in all directions at all hours. So while loading platforms can be shared—the

four o'clock limited to Chicago can use the same platform as the four-thirty Washington express and the six o'clock Philadelphia local—other station facilities are set apart to serve the needs of commuter and long-distance passengers separately.

BAY AREA TERMINALS

For many years, the Southern Pacific was California's transportation monopoly. The railroad had a stranglehold on nearly all rail lines in the state. Its headquarters stood on Market Street in San Francisco, a short distance from the waterfront. The ferry building was designated milepost 0, and every point on the Southern Pacific's vast empire was measured from there—which is curious, since the Southern Pacific never had any tracks to this point! Its San Francisco terminal at Third and Townsend Streets was several blocks away. This station served Peninsula commuter trains and service southward (east on Southern Pacific's strictly bi-direction timetable) to Los Angeles, and more out-of-the-way points, like Santa Cruz and Monterey, which were reached by branch lines. However, the majority of long-distance traffic came via the overland route by way of Utah and Donner Pass, so passenger trains from the East terminated in Oakland on a pier known as the Oakland Mole, which extended nearly a mile into San Francisco Bay. Passengers destined for San Francisco—where the majority went at that time—would transfer to a ferry for a ride across the bay. Trains stopped using the Mole by 1960.

Southern Pacific's Third & Townsend Station survived longer than its peer across the bay. Although many Mission-style railroad stations were constructed around the Southwest and California, Third & Townsend was one of the most impressive examples of that style.

HOBOKEN TERMINAL

In Hoboken, New Jersey, on the west bank of the Hudson River opposite Manhattan, sits the last great waterfront railroad station in North America. All the waterfront passenger terminals in other parts of the country have long since gone. The old Delaware, Lackawanna & Western Hoboken Terminal was once one of five huge terminals on the New Jersey side of the river. The wide Hudson River presented a formidable barrier against direct rail service to

San Francisco's Mission Revival–style terminal at Third and Townsend streets was built in 1915 in conjunction with the Panama-Pacific Exposition, San Francisco's celebration of the Panama Canal opening. It was demolished in the mid-1970s and replaced with a spartan commuter-rail terminal at Fourth and Townsend.

New York City from the south and west. To serve America's largest city, railroads built terminals along the waterfront opposite Manhattan and ferried passengers across the river.

The present Hoboken terminal was built in 1907 to replace an older facility. Shortly before midnight on August 7, 1905, a fire broke out aboard the ferry boat *Hopatcong*, which was docked at the Lackawanna's slips. The sensational fire spread rapidly, and soon the entire waterfront was ablaze, the flames clearly visible from Manhattan. By the time the fire was extinguished, the Lackawanna Railroad's gateway to New York City had been razed. The railroad rebuilt its largest terminal, and the new facility was far better than the one it replaced. The Lackawanna was a very profitable line, and the company wished to display its wealth, so it hired Kenneth Murchison, a well-known New York architect, to design its new terminal. Murchison, who had studied in Paris, created a glorious Beaux Arts–style building. Its 750-foot-long (228.5m) head house is ornately decorated with sheets of copper. The station's magnificent waiting room is among the most elegant in the New York metropolitan area. Its great Tiffany glass ceiling rises fifty feet (15m) above the floor, and the walls are made of fine limestone decorated with bronze and iron. Originally the terminal featured a 250-foot-tall (76m) clock tower, which was later removed.

Perhaps the Hoboken terminal's most important feature is its train shed. Rather than employ a large, arched, balloon-type shed, Lincoln Bush, Lackawanna's chief engineer, designed a radical new type of cantilevered train shed made of steel, glass, and concrete. This was the first shed of its type, and it quickly proved its value since it was less costly to build and far less costly to maintain than traditional train sheds. Soon Bush train sheds supplanted balloon-type arches on new terminals around the United States and Canada. But today, Hoboken's Bush shed is among the few remaining of its type.

Hoboken Terminal's role has evolved over its long life. When it was built it served both commuters and long-distance passengers. The Lackawanna's commuter lines, serving Montclair, Dover, and rural Gladstone, were among the best patronized in northern New Jersey. The railroad's long-distance trains ran to Scranton, Pennsylvania, and Binghamton and Buffalo, New York. Its most famous passenger train, the Phoebe Snow, ran the length of the railroad to Buffalo. The railroad skillfully pro-

The former Delaware, Lackawanna & Western's Hoboken Terminal is the last active passenger terminal on the New Jersey waterfront opposite New York City. It is also one of the last great American passenger terminals. The copper plate used to decorate the station was left over from building the Statue of Liberty.

In recent years the main waiting room of Hoboken Terminal has been restored to its former glory, and the station again displays the Beaux Arts design of Kenneth Murchison in full splendor. Hoboken Terminal serves commuter trains operated by NJ Transit.

moted this train with an advertising campaign that involved Phoebe Snow, a caricature of the train's persona.

Originally, nearly all passengers passing through Hoboken would transfer from trains to double-decked ferries. There were six ferry slips, with service to three different points in Manhattan: Christopher Street, Twenty-third Street, and Barclay Street. In 1908, passengers were given an alternative to the perils of the river crossing when the Hudson & Manhattan rapid transit tunnels opened under the river. Although the new electric subways offered swift, safe, and comfortable passage to Manhattan, for years many Lackawanna passengers remained loyal to the ferries. The ferries provided more direct service, and the ferry ride was included in the train fare. Nonetheless, patronage gradually dwindled and, in the late 1960s, the ferries finally succumbed to modernization. Yet, after more than a twenty-year lapse, ferry service resumed in the early 1990s.

In the 1930s, the Lackawanna electrified its suburban commuter lines. It is said that electricity pioneer Thomas Edison personally operated one of the first new electric trains to Hoboken Terminal. While passenger railroading suffered a slow decline after World War II, the Hoboken Terminal received a boost in 1956 when the Lackawanna's neighbor and longtime arch-competitor, Erie Railroad, moved its suburban commuter trains to Hoboken from its own Pavonia Terminal in Jersey City in order to cut costs. This was the first step toward consolidation; in 1960, the two railroads formally merged to form the Erie-Lackawanna Railroad. Long-distance service to Hoboken lingered until January 1970, when the last intercity train on the Erie-Lackawanna was discontinued. Since that time, Hoboken has survived solely as a commuter terminal.

During the 1970s, Hoboken Terminal was recognized as a historic landmark. In the 1980s, it was restored. It has retained much of its origi-

nal charm and looks very much the way it did on opening day in 1907, although the trains today are very modern. Hoboken is not a museum and continues to serve as a vital passenger terminal. One can still board trains for Suffern and Port Jervis, New York, and Dover, Netcong, and Hackettstown, New Jersey. In the mid-1990s, Hoboken's role was altered: NJ Transit built a connection between the old Lackawanna main line and the Northeast Corridor route, which allowed trains to operate directly from Hoboken to Penn Station in Newark and down the New Jersey shore to Bay Head, service that was never possible when the Lackawanna ran the show. Hoboken Terminal has also lost a great deal of through traffic, however, because many of the electric trains that once served the terminal now operate via a new connection at Harrison directly into Pennsylvania Station in Manhattan. Still, Hoboken survives as one of America's greatest railroad terminals.

LEFT: *Koblenz, located at the confluence of the Rhine and Moselle rivers, is one of the oldest cities in Germany. The depot serves several important rail routes—trains from all over Germany stop here.* BELOW: *Several of Spain's high-speed electric AVE trains pause beneath the train shed in Madrid. This modern facility was built to replace an older station and is linked to Madrid's other terminal by a modern tunnel below the city center.* RIGHT: *London's Charing Cross Station is a terminal situated on the Thames River. Originally built in the 1860s to serve the South Eastern Railway, it was modernized and redeveloped in the 1980s. To support the new structure above the platforms, large piles were driven deep into the clay below the station.*

ABOVE: *The small interurban terminal at Mishima, Japan, is typical of stub-end facilities. Tracks come into the station from only one direction and stop at bumping posts. Since this is the end of the line, and most passengers using the interurban electric line use this station, the stub-end arrangement is a very efficient use of terminal space.* RIGHT: *St. Louis Union Station, designed by Theodore C. Link and Edward B. Cameron, was built in the Norman Revival style between 1891 and 1895 and made of Missouri granite.*

LEFT: *The train shed at the Gare du Nord in Paris was designed by Léonce Reynaud and built between 1861 and 1865. The shed is a truss-type supported by brackets; its construction is similar to that of the shed at Liverpool Street in London illustrated on page 70.* BELOW: *The arched train shed in Frankfort, Germany is considered one of the greatest in Europe. It was completed in 1888 and is still in use today.* OPPOSITE: *The train shed in York, England, built between 1871 and 1877, is immediately identifiable because it is situated on a curve. Since this photo was taken, the track arrangement was modified to accommodate electrification and the traditional look of the station has changed.*

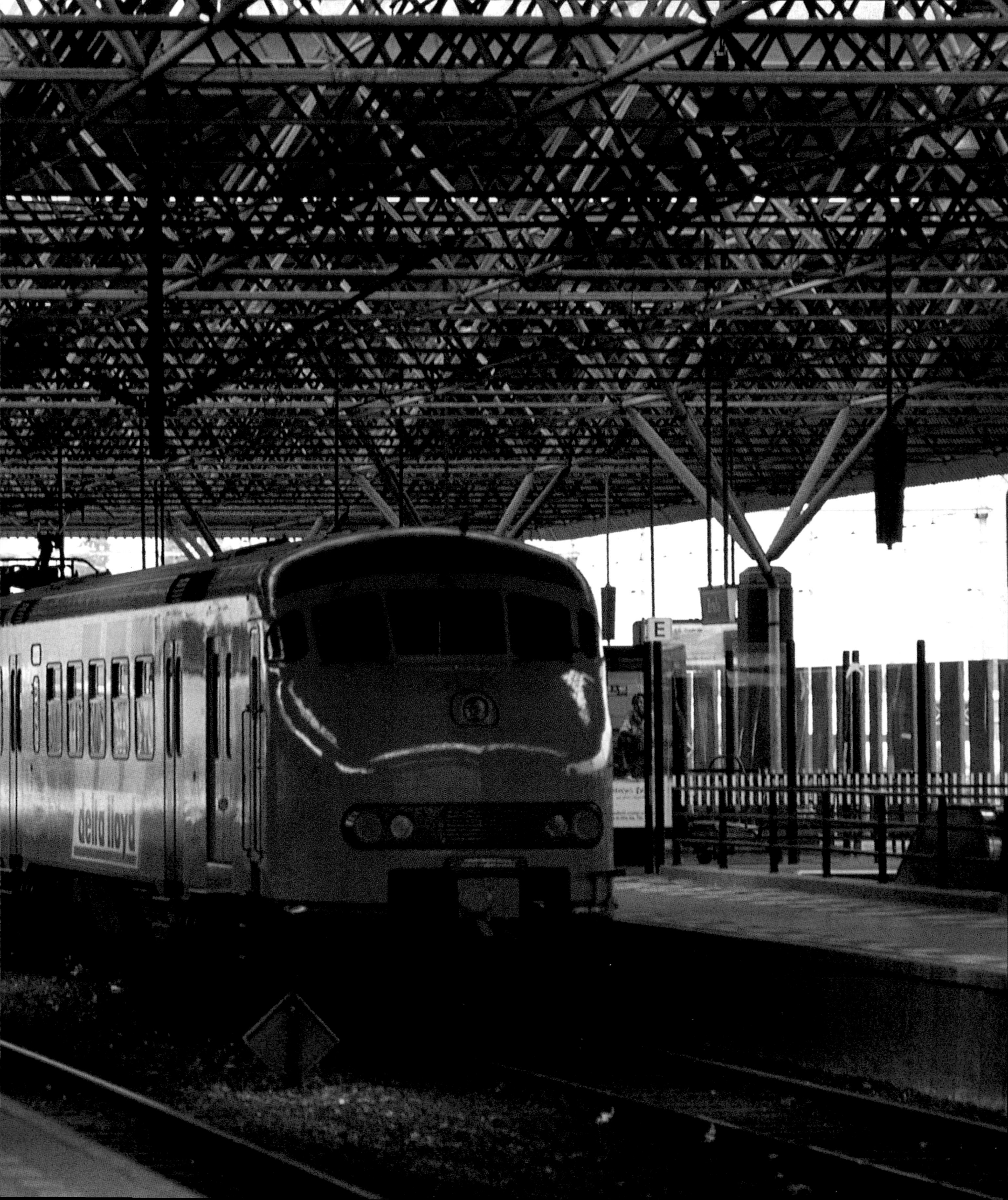
E
delta lloyd

PAGES 68-69: *The railway network in the Netherlands is among the most efficient in the Western world. Dutch trains run at reasonably high speeds, on frequent intervals to most cities, all day long. A commuter train pauses below the modern train shed at Breda, in the Netherlands.* LEFT: *London's Liverpool Street Station was designed by Edward Wilson, a Great Eastern Railway engineer, and built between 1874 and 1894. Recently, British Rail reconstructed the station and brought it up to modern standards while retaining elements of its original construction.* ABOVE: *Shimobe, Japan, is a popular resort destination, and as a result it has a distinctive, although somewhat diminutive, railway depot. In Japan many smaller stations emulate pagoda architecture. Most larger Japanese stations are more modern in their appearance.*

ABOVE: *One of the few surviving American train sheds, which now shelters a lagoon and urban park, is the one at St. Louis Union Station. This enormous shed was built in several spans and is 600 feet (183m) wide. It was very similar to the vast, now-vanished shed at South Station in Boston, Massachusetts.* RIGHT: *The tremendous balloon train shed at Antwerp, Belgium, is 212 (65m) feet wide. It was inspired by the Crystal Palace in London and features exceptionally well executed Art Nouveau ironwork. Like many terminals, it features a stub-end design. Through trains must travel in reverse back to the main line before continuing their journey.*

CHAPTER 4

CLASSIC STATIONS

Whereas many areas of the world have marched blindly into the modern world, replacing classic buildings with modern ones without concern for aesthetics or history, some areas have not. In some places, country farms with rustic barns and traditional covered bridges abound. Stone walls are more common than convenience stores and, for the most part, the landscape looks much the way it did fifty years ago. Not that there are no modern edifices, but the character of the places appears to have been relatively unaffected by contemporary trends and the buildings of yesteryear have remained as they were.

stops here twice a day. Passengers may ride up from Bellows Falls and lay over between runs, or they may board here for the train ride. The Green Mountain Railroad still operates a daily freight train from Bellows Falls to Rutland. And, in a timeless pattern followed here for more than a century, the passenger train will take the siding (switch off the main line) to get out of the way at Chester to allow the freight train to safely run around it.

Further along the Green Mountain Railroad is another fine station, at Ludlow. Trains stop there several times a year when the railroad runs excursions from Bellows Falls.

PAGE 74: *Vermont, known for its pastoral scenery and rustic covered bridges, also has many classic railroad stations. The former Central Vermont Railway station in Shelburne, Vermont, is now part of the Shelburne Museum—a 45-acre (18ha) site that is home to thirty-seven historic buildings.* PAGE 75: *The former New Haven Railroad station in West Cornwall is one of many extant railroad stations in Connecticut's scenic Housatonic River Valley.* ABOVE: *Despite the unavoidable presence of modern automobiles, the depot at Chester, Vermont, is picture perfect. The nicely restored depot was built in 1872 and still serves seasonal Green Mountain Railroad passenger trains.* OPPOSITE: *Baltimore's Penn Station is a true classic and an active station as well, hosting dozens of daily Amtrak and MARC commuter-rail trains. It is the work of Kenneth Murchison, the architect responsible for Hoboken Terminal.*

BALTIMORE'S PENNSYLVANIA STATION

One of the most attractive stations on the Northeast Corridor is Baltimore's Pennsylvania Station, which opened on September 15, 1911. In *I Remember Pennsy*, Don Wood describes the station as Pennsy's (the Pennsylvania Railroad) Acropolis, aptly evoking the station's impressive Beaux Arts, Neoclassical design. The style is typical of architecture designed by Kenneth Murchison, who is also responsible for the stations in Hoboken, New Jersey, and Scranton, Pennsylvania. The Baltimore Pennsylvania Station replaced a depot at the same location that had been built in 1886 by Pennsylvania Railroad's predecessor, Northern Central. The old depot had become inadequate for the volume of traffic that it needed to handle. The new station, a relatively large through station which was known as Baltimore Union Station, was served by three subsidiaries of the Pennsylvania Railroad and the Western Maryland.

Baltimore's Penn Station is a building of moderate size. It is four stories tall, and the two upper floors are used primarily as offices. While not nearly as massive as other depots in large eastern cities—Penn Station's two-story main waiting room is only sixty-five feet (20m) wide by ninety-five feet (29m) deep—it displays an architectural perfection rarely seen in American depots of this size. The principal structure is made of pink granite quarried at Milford, Massachusetts. The interior is Pentelic (from Pentelikon Mountain in Greece) and Sicilian marble. A balcony, which wraps around the second story, is supported by rows of Doric columns. Above, three intricate stained-glass skylights bathe the waiting room in soft pastel light. Classical stone relief sculpture embellishes

VERMONT'S GEMS

This applies especially to Vermont's depots. Not demolished in the name of progress, not considered outmoded, unneeded, or in the way, country stations in Vermont have been maintained and preserved, and a number of classic structures still host daily or seasonal passenger trains.

Bellows Falls, a handsome village in southern Vermont along the Connecticut River, features a solid-brick railroad station once served by trains of the Rutland, Boston & Maine and Central Vermont railroads. The station originally had canopies, which now have been removed, over its platforms to protect passengers from the weather. Today, Bellows Falls is one of the few stations in the United States

where one can make a connection between Amtrak and a privately operated passenger train. The station hosts the daily Amtrak Vermonter, a connecting bus service, and the seasonal Green Mountain Railroad excursion trains that operate along the old Rutland tracks to Chester, Vermont.

Chester is the location of a beautifully restored depot built in 1872. It is a quintessential small-town New England station, complete with a semaphore train order signal, which was once a standard feature at depots throughout North America. The station is constructed of red brick with arched windows, corbeled cornices, and a classic bracketed canopy that wraps around the building. From June to mid-October, the historic Green Mountain passenger train

the station's concourse, which is conveniently situated directly above tracks that are located in a trench below street level. The principal parts of the station—waiting rooms, ticket counters, and baggage facilities—are at street level. The station is laid out so that passengers have only to walk a short distance from the tracks to reach the exit. In this regard, designers of larger stations could have learned from Murchison's example. When the Baltimore station was new, John Droege noted in his book *Passenger Terminals and Trains*, it was the only station with depressed tracks to have a Bush train shed. Today, it is among the last to employ this type of shed.

During World War II, the station's glass skylights had been covered for fear of air raids.

In the 1980s, these skylights were restored to their former glory as part of a general refurbishing and rededication. Now, in many respects, the station is as beautiful and vital as it was fifty years ago. In the late 1920s and early 1930s, the Pennsylvania Railroad electrified its New York to Washington route, which runs through Baltimore. This speeded up passenger service, and today the terminal is served by dozens of Amtrak trains operating on the Northeast Corridor between Boston and Washington, D.C., and by several long-distance trains, including several to Florida and New Orleans. Maryland-sponsored commuter trains running between Perryville, Maryland, and Washington, D.C., also stop at Baltimore.

CALIFORNIA STATIONS

Sacramento

Sacramento was the original western terminus of the first transcontinental railroad, which was completed on May 10, 1869. By the 1870s, the Central Pacific had built lines to the Bay Area and southward through the Central Valley, but Sacramento remained one of the railroad's most important facilities. In 1879, a large arcade-style station with a train shed—a rarity for the western United States, where there is relatively little precipitation—was constructed. The Central Pacific was gradually folded into the Southern Pacific, and, by the turn of the century, the Southern Pacific had become the most powerful transportation force in the West. As people flocked to California from the East, the railroad's freight and passenger traffic grew enormously. By the 1920s, the Sacramento depot was wholly inadequate for the traffic it was required to handle. In addition to the transcontinental traffic coming over Donner Pass, traffic from Oregon, California's Central Valley, and Southern California poured through Sacramento. From every direction, traffic was booming with no end in sight.

In the mid-1920s, a new station was built at 401 I Street as part of a new terminal complex that cost more than $2 million. Its architects had worked for McKim, Mead and White in New York City, the same firm that had designed the impressive New York Pennsylvania Station. The new three-story Sacramento station opened on February 27, 1925, and, while it is not nearly as large an undertaking, in subtle ways its Renaissance Revival style resembles the original New York building. The Sacramento station features a grand waiting room with marble floors, mahogany woodwork, and a domed ceiling sixty feet (18m) high. Above the waiting room were railroad divisional offices and train dispatching facilities. The station reflects the wealth of the great Southern Pacific in every detail. Waiting passengers can rest on large, solid wooden benches, each with Southern Pacific's highly detailed Sunset Route emblem carved into the ends. The exterior is faced with handsome Italian sienna brick and terra cotta, in the style of other large Southern Pacific stations. But if the style alone does not tip off the casual observer, there can be no doubt as to whose station this is: atop the station, carved in large letters, are the words "Southern

The Southern Pacific Station in Sacramento, California, retains most of the features of a classic railroad station and displays a distinctive character that many city stations have lost. The famous MacQuarrie mural of Leland Stanford can be seen above the doorways on the left.

One of the best remaining examples of a Mission Revival--style station is the San Diego, California, depot built in 1915. The Santa Fe Railroad's distinctive logo is set in stone on both of the station's towers. The San Diego trolley, which operates several lines in the city, stops in front of the station, giving rail passengers a practical mass-transit option.

Pacific Lines." It is unlikely that any traveler searching to travel with Southern Pacific's competition, the Western Pacific, would have mistakenly passed through this building's doors.

Perhaps Southern Pacific's Sacramento station is best known for the large mural by artist John A. MacQuarrie depicting the Central Pacific's ground-breaking ceremony in 1863. In this painting, the railroad's illustrious president—and California governor—Leland Stanford is seen moving the first shovelful of earth. It is said that six years after the ground-

breaking, Stanford tapped the final golden spike into place, connecting his line with that of the Union Pacific at Promontory, Utah, thus completing the first transcontinental railroad route. It is also said that Stanford was later criticized by fellow Central Pacific owner Charlie Crocker for having moved the first earth and tapped the final spike but doing little else toward the construction of the line! Today Sacramento's station is among the finest in California, and it has recently enjoyed a renaissance; it now serves nearly a dozen trains daily.

San Diego

San Diego Union Station is the best example extant of Spanish-style depot architecture in California. It was built in 1915 in conjunction with the California-Pacific Exposition, which celebrated the opening of the Panama Canal. Designed to handle heavy crowds, the station is constructed of steel, brick, and concrete, with a stucco exterior and a red-tiled roof. The entrance is a great archway flanked by Moorish towers, each of which sports a Santa Fe

Railroad logo in colored tiles. San Diego was served by both the Santa Fe and, until 1951, the Southern Pacific subsidiary San Diego & Arizona (later San Diego & Arizona Eastern). As with many Santa Fe stations, San Diego Union featured a Harvey House restaurant.

Like many California communities, San Diego has experienced a rail renaissance. The depot was restored in 1982, and today it is a principal intermodal transportation hub. Weekdays, Amtrak operates nine San Diego-to-Los Angeles San Diegans, some of which continue north through Los Angeles to Santa Barbara and San Luis Obispo. The station is also served by Coaster commuter trains, which began operating in 1995, and the local San Diego trolley.

CONNECTICUT'S CLASSICS

New London

Situated conveniently between the waterfront and downtown neighborhoods, New London Union Station has seen more than 110 years of continuous use as a railroad depot. It was designed by Henry Hobson Richardson between 1885 and 1886 to replace an earlier station, which had burned down. The new New London Union was the largest and also the last railroad station that Richardson designed; it was completed in 1887, after his death in the summer of 1886. It is made of red brick, features the classic Richardsonian hipped roof, and employs ornamental patterns in the exterior brickwork. The main entrance from the street is decorated by an archway of molded bricks, above which the words "Union Railroad Station" are spelled out in brick. A large, gabled peak, punctuated by rows of three distinctive vertical windows, dominates the center of the building.

Union Station was built and owned by the New London Northern, and the second floor housed the railroad's divisional offices, dispatching center, and operator's offices. The passenger facilities—which included a waiting room, restaurant, telegraph office, and baggage area—were shared with the New Haven Railroad. In 1937, the New London Northern's successor, the Central Vermont Railway, moved its offices out of the handsome depot to a smaller structure nearby. After World War II, the Central Vermont discontinued regular passenger service, although the station continued to be

New London Union Station, in Connecticut, sits on the waterfront. It was designed by H.H. Richardson and built for the New London Northern line. Richardson designed many fine railroad stations, including the Union Station at Palmer, Massachusetts (shown on pages 44–45).

served by New Haven's passenger trains. The New Haven was absorbed by the Penn Central in 1969, and in 1971 passenger services were conveyed to Amtrak. New London's railroad station narrowly escaped destruction during urban renewal programs of the early 1970s and was renovated in the mid-1970s. Today, the Union Railroad Station is the centerpiece of a revitalized New London. Amtrak occupies a large area on the first floor, and the rest of the station is used as office space. Some one dozen Amtrak trains operating between Boston and Washington, D.C., stop here daily, and ferry service to Long Island is available from a nearby pier.

Hartford

Located downtown, near the state capitol, Hartford's railroad station is a superb example of Richardsonian Romanesque architecture. It was originally planned by George Keller, executed by Shepley, Rutan & Coolidge, and constructed in 1889 by Orland Norcross. It is made from brownstone quarried at Portland, Connecticut.

The station was remodeled in 1914, following a devastating fire. A mural over the platform entrance depicting both steam and electrically powered trains reflects the New Haven's onetime ambition to electrify all its principal lines. The railroad never achieved this goal, for the Hartford route was never electrified.

The Hartford station features a large, two-story central waiting room, with office space, shops, and a restaurant on either side. At one time, four tracks served the station, but today there is just one. In recent years, the Hartford station was renovated. Today, it serves as an intermodal transportation hub. A dozen Amtrak trains daily connect Hartford with many other Northeastern communities. Other nearby stations have also been renovated. At Windsor, Connecticut, Amtrak serves a handsome brick station that was completely restored in the mid-1980s. Another fine station is located south of Hartford at Wallingford.

LONDON'S ST. PANCRAS

London's railway terminals are among the best known in the world. Waterloo, Paddington, King's Cross, Liverpool Street, and Victoria are all outstanding classic railway stations, but it is St. Pancras that deserves the highest architectural praise. When it opened in 1869, a long of railway station innovation in England came to a close. St. Pancras' two principal components, the world's first great arched train shed and an elaborate head house, were designed by different men and completed at different times. William Henry Barlow designed the shed with the help of R. Ordish. The Butterley Iron Company manufactured the great cast-iron arches used to support the single-span shed— 689 feet (210m) long, 240 feet (73m) wide, and roughly 100 feet (30.5m) tall at the apex. It is one of the finest railway sheds ever built and among the largest remaining in regular use.

The head house was designed by one of England's best known architects, Giles Gilbert Scott, and is an outstanding example of Victorian Gothic Revival architecture. Its elaborately ornate façade makes liberal use of columns, arches, gables, and towers. Londoners joke about the fact that it has often been mistaken for a church.

The station's builder, the Midland Railway, wished to appeal to Britain's upper class and no expense was to be spared for their comfort. Importantly though, St. Pancras, like many early train stations, was considered to be more than just a terminal for passengers' convenience. It was a status symbol that reflected both the railroad's success and that of imperial England. It was built to inspire awe and wonder. Today, 120 years after its opening, it remains one of the world's greatest train stations.

Designed in 1889 by H. H. Richardson's architectural successors, Shepley, Rutan & Coolidge, the railroad station in Hartford, Connecticut, is an excellent example of the Richardsonian Romanesque style popular in the 1880s and 1890s.

ABOVE: *One of England's most famous and most distinctive stations is St. Pancras. The large balloon shed was opened in 1868, while the Midland Grand Hotel, the head house for the railroad station, designed by Sir Gilbert Scott, was added in 1873.* RIGHT: *The design of Central Station in Helsinki, Finland, was the result of a competition won by the great Finnish architect Eliel Saarinen, who studied stations in Germany, England, and Scotland. Completed in 1914, the station did not open until after World War I.*

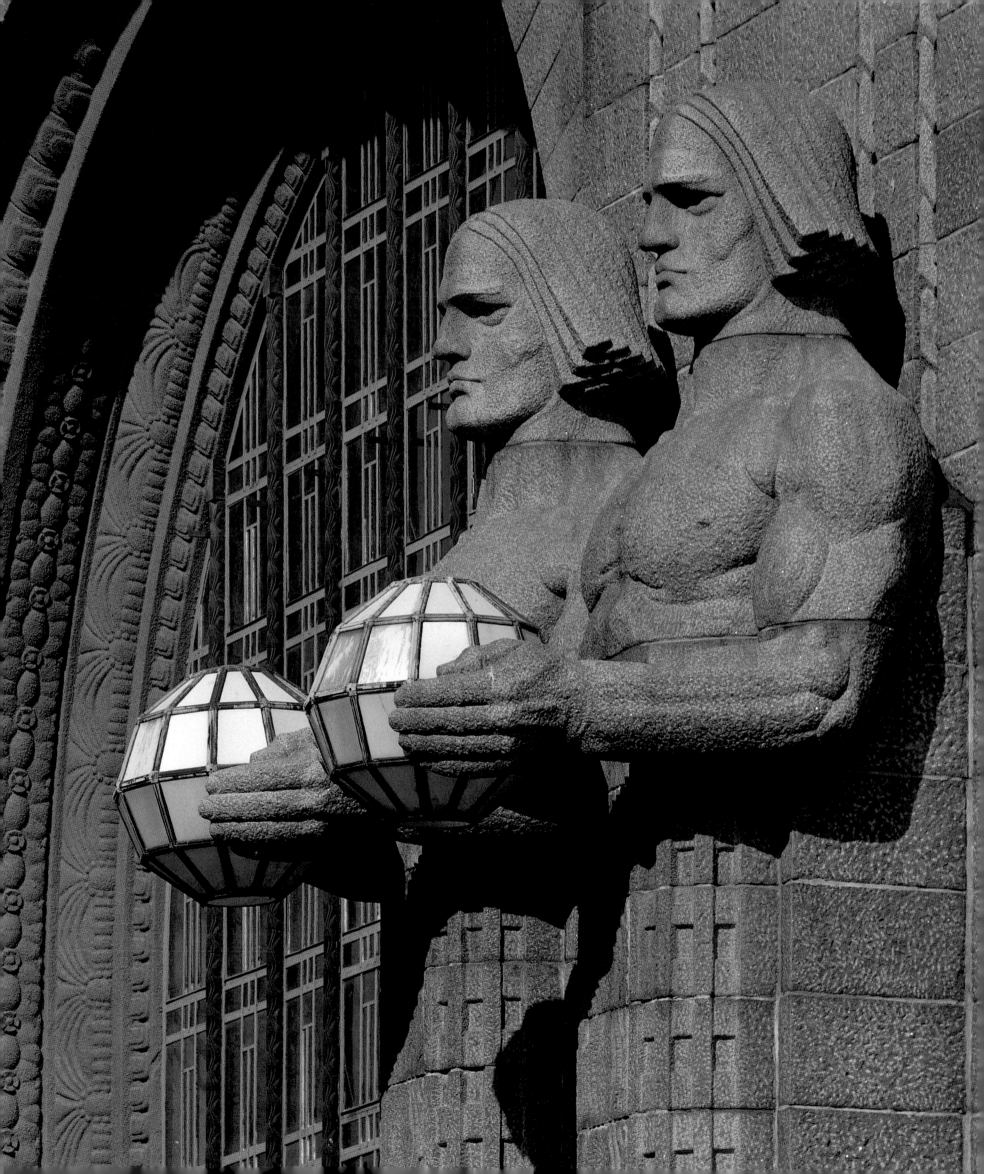

OPPOSITE: *Hartford's ornate brownstone station was the work of Shepley, Rutan & Coolidge, the architectural firm that succeeded H. H. Richardson. The station sits in the shadow of the Connecticut State Capitol.* ABOVE: *One of Connecticut's many active railroad stations is this Victorian classic in Windsor in the Connecticut River Valley. It was recently refurbished and now serves a dozen daily Amtrak trains.*

PAGES 86–87: *Canaan Union Station is one of several fine stations located along the Housatonic Railroad in western Connecticut. It was built in the 1890s and later served two routes of the New Haven Railroad. Its three-story tower is an excellent example of Gothic Revival architecture. Regular passenger service to Canaan ended in 1971.* OPPOSITE: *Union Station in Nashville, Tennessee, was built in 1900 for the Tennessee Central and Louisville & Nashville lines. Designed by Richard Montfort, it is an excellent example of Richardsonian Romanesque architecture.* ABOVE: *The classic station in Nice, France, is among the survivors of World War II. Considered military targets, many great railway stations were destroyed or heavily damaged during the war.*

PAGES 90–91: *Huntingdon, Pennsylvania, a large town in the central part of the state and its county's seat, was also at one time the junction between the Middle Division of the Pennsylvania Railroad and the Huntingdon & Broad Top. The large two-story brick depot was restored to its original Victorian-era paint scheme in the early 1990s.* ABOVE: *The Amherst, Massachusetts, depot is a handsome, well-kept station. Twice every day, including holidays, the little depot sees a flurry of activity when the trains stop—around lunch time for the southbound Vermonter, and again in the late afternoon for the ame train northbound. This station originally served trains of the New London Northern and later Central Vermont Railway.* LEFT: *On a clear April 1997 evening the Hale-Bopp comet glowed in the starry sky above the Amherst station.*

OPPOSITE: *Baltimore's Pennsylvania Station displays an exceptionally efficient station layout—passengers have a very short walk from the street to the tracks. The colorful skylights pictured here were covered over during World War II due to fear of air raids.* ABOVE: *The Baltimore & Ohio station at Point of Rocks, Maryland, is located at the junction between the "old main line" and the present-day main line. The depot was built in 1875 and serves as a commuter stop for MARC trains, which provide local rail service in eastern Maryland.*

CHAPTER 5

GONE BUT NOT FORGOTTEN

Some of the greatest stations the world has ever seen are no longer standing. Changes in corporate policies, decling or evolving railroad ridership patterns, and urban renewal combined with changing attitudes toward architectural design have contributed to the loss of some of the world's most imposing and beautiful railway stations. Some of the best-known and finest stations were demolished during the 1950s, 1960s, and 1970s. Many small-town stations were bulldozed without a second thought; however, the destruction of well-known city terminals created great controversy. Some of these great stations are still remembered today.

PAGE 96: *The magnificent station building at Broad Street in Philadelphia was built in 1891 and served the Pennsylvania Railroad for more than sixty years. In 1952 the building was demolished; had it been preserved it would likely have been heralded as one of Philadelphia's great landmarks.* PAGE 97: *Pennsylvania Railroad's Suburban Station in Philadelphia was built to replace Broad Street Station.* ABOVE: *London's Euston Station was best known for its Greek Revival arch. Plans to demolish this landmark caused tremendous public controversy, but, despite the protests, the arch was torn down in 1961. Its loss is still remembered today.*

LONDON'S EUSTON STATION

Euston Station opened in 1838 as London's first main line railway terminal. It originally served the London & Birmingham Railway and was the prototypical iron train shed, planned by British railway pioneer Robert Stephenson and designed by Charles Fox. This simple iron shed was 200 feet (61m) long and built in two spans. While its technologically significant shed had a great effect on future station design, Euston's most famous attribute was not its shed but its arch, a Greek Revival portico supported by four Doric columns, which was designed by the duke of Wellington's architect, Philip Hardwick. Hardwick's son, Philip Charles, designed the station's waiting area, which was known as the Great Hall. It was not completed until 1849, a decade after the rest of the station was finished. A statue of George Stephenson, Robert's father and one of the inventors of the steam locomotive, presided over the hall.

Euston retained its original character throughout its long life, although numerous modifications and renovations expanded the station. Several plans for its replacement had been drafted over the years but always failed to come to fruition—until the late 1950s, when a new station was finally designed and approved to take the place of the 120-year-old landmark. Unfortunately, this new, larger station did not retain Euston's historic architecture. The arch and the Great Hall would have to go. The public outcry over the proposed destruction of the greatly loved relic was enormous, and a great controversy was aired in the London press. The protests went to the highest levels of government, but pleas to Prime Minister Harold Macmillan to save Euston proved futile. In late

1961, Euston was demolished. A modern station, completed in 1968, took its place. Although this new station is a more efficient terminal, thirty years after old Euston's demise, Londoners still bemoan its loss. Indeed, it seems criminal that such an architectural landmark could be destroyed in the name of progress.

PHILADELPHIA'S BROAD STREET STATION

At the end of the nineteenth century, Philadelphia was the heart and brain of the Pennsylvania Railroad, one of the most powerful organizations in the United States. Philadelphia was the site of both the company's headquarters and the busiest passenger terminal on the system. In 1881, the Pennsylvania Railroad constructed a gargantuan train shed to serve Philadelphia. It was more than just impressive, it was *the* largest single-span train shed ever built—300 feet (91.5m) wide and 108 feet (33m) high. To reach the shed, Pennsylvania Railroad trains ran along a solid, multiple-track, elevated structure called the Chinese Wall. Ten years later, the railroad built a terminal building to augment the great shed. Broad Street Station, designed by Frank Furness, combined the company offices with a large station building. This exceptionally ornate, massive structure was the apogee of Victorian station building in America. Its impressive stone façade reflected the awesome industrial might of the Pennsylvania Railroad.

Despite all its grandeur, Broad Street had several failings. By 1910, the twenty-year-old structure was straining under an exceptional volume of traffic, four times what it had been designed to handle. Its sixteen tracks served nearly six hundred daily trains and some eighty thousand passengers. In 1915, Pennsylvania Railroad electrified the terminal and several suburban routes in an effort to increase the station's capacity. Because of its downtown location, the station was hemmed in on all sides, making expansion difficult. Perhaps its greatest downfall was that it was a stub-end terminal on what became Pennsylvania Railroad's principal through route between New York and Washington. By the 1920s, the through trains of the railroad's New York-to-Washington corridor bypassed Broad Street, stopping at a small station at Thirty-third Street on the western side of the Schuylkill River, a distance from downtown.

The beginning of the end of Broad Street Station came in the early morning hours of June

11, 1923, when fire spread throughout the shed and consumed it. The railroad swiftly rebuilt the terminal with incredible vigor. A week after the catastrophic fire, service to Broad Street had been completely restored. However, the shed was weakened by the blaze and had to be dismantled, so plans were soon afoot to replace Broad Street Station. Between 1928 and 1933, Pennsylvania Railroad built a large through station at Thirtieth Street and an adjacent station above it for suburban trains, as part of the New York-to-Washington electrification. The upper-level spur served a new underground terminal adjacent to Broad Street, called Suburban Station, and the old Broad Street Station itself on its Chinese Wall. Broad Street survived with this temporary connection into the 1950s, served by the New York Clockers, whose new GG1 electric passenger locomotives could not run into the new Suburban Station.

Finally on April 27, 1952, Broad Street was closed. Sadly, the station was destroyed rather than adapted to another use. The shortsighted thinking of the time justified the destruction of a beautiful architectural monument as progress. Pennsylvania Railroad President James "Big Jim" Symes excused his audacious act of corporate vandalism in a public statement, saying, "Old Broad Street Station was constructed 70 years ago. . . . When it was built it was one of the finest passenger terminals in the world. It has served the City of Philadelphia well. . . . It is an old landmark that many of us will dislike seeing go: but *remember*—it is being replaced with Pennsylvania Station at 30th Street, one of the most modern, practical, and beautiful passenger terminals in the world—barring none."

Unfortunately Symes' reign of terror on the Pennsylvania Railroad's architectural landmarks would not end with the destruction of Broad Street. Before he was through, Pennsylvania Railroad's crown jewel, Pennsylvania Station, New York, would fall to the wreckers.

NEW YORK'S PENNSYLVANIA STATION

Prior to the turn of the century, the desire for a direct entrance to the United States' largest city tormented Pennsylvania Railroad management. This goal was unachievable because the mighty Hudson River presented an insurmountable obstacle. To reach New York, Pennsylvania Railroad passengers rode to a large terminal on the New Jersey shore called Exchange Place and then transferred to ferries, which brought them

across the river. The ferry ride was anything but glamorous, and, in the winter, it was downright unpleasant. Further aggravating the situation, Pennsylvania's archrival, the New York Central & Hudson River Railroad, did have a direct rail connection to New York City by way of a Hudson River crossing at Albany. Its handsome Grand Central Station sat in the center of Manhattan at Forty-second Street. Alexander Cassatt, a long-time Pennsylvania Railroad director, found this situation intolerable.

In 1899, Cassatt became president of the Pennsylvania Railroad and quickly exerted his new authority toward realizing his goal of a terminal in New York City. It was his dream to build a new railroad structure that would dwarf any terminal that had been constructed in the United States. But the problem of how to get his trains to Manhattan still had to be solved. In 1901, Cassatt was in Paris visiting his sister Mary Cassatt, the famous Impressionist painter, when he went to the recently opened Gare d'Orsay. There he witnessed firsthand the advantages of using electric locomotives rather than steam, while experiencing the splendor of one of Europe's finest railway stations. The French had electrified a short section of railroad, allowing trains to pass through a tunnel directly into the station. There was no separate shed; the station and platforms were a single, integrated facility. These electric trains were notably quieter and cleaner than traditional, steam-powered trains.

Cassatt saw the Gare d'Orsay as the prototype for New York's Pennsylvania Station. He hired his friend Charles McKim, one of America's foremost architects of the French Beaux Arts school, to design the station, and he set Pennsylvania Railroad's engineers to work on a complex network of tunnels that would connect New Jersey, Manhattan, and Long Island, and on a bridge from Manhattan to the Bronx on the mainland, which would allow service to New England. Pennsylvania Station was not to be a stub-end terminal like Grand Central, but a magnificent through station.

Inspired by Cassatt's vision, McKim designed one of the most outstanding structures ever to be built in the United States. McKim's model for the main waiting room was the ancient Baths of Caracalla in Rome. He used the same variety of stone as the Romans had, travertine marble. Enormous Corinthian columns, more than sixty feet (18m) high, supported the vaulted ceiling that rose to a height of 150 feet (45.5m). The Seventh Avenue façade featured a row of immense Doric columns of

pink marble from Milford, Massachusetts. The concourse was in a different style, with a tremendous glass-and-steel roof supported by rows of tall steel columns in the spirit of London's Crystal Palace.

A famous sculptor, Adolph A. Weinman, was commissioned to create great stone ornaments for the complex. He crafted eagles—the imperial symbols of ancient Rome and Byzantium—and sculpted beautiful maidens representing day and night to decorate the main waiting room. The building was designed with multiple entrances and large, wide corridors to allow for a smooth flow of traffic. In the Beaux Arts tradition, McKim built the great station to be functional as well as beautiful.

After five years of excavation, tunnel boring, and concrete pouring for the platform and yard level, construction of the building began in 1909. When it was completed in 1911, it was acclaimed as the handsomest train station in the world, a monument to the Pennsylvania Railroad, and a gift to the city of New York. Unfortunately, neither Cassatt nor McKim ever saw the palace they had long dreamed of; Cassatt had died in 1906, and McKim had passed away two years later.

By the 1950s, the once robust Pennsylvania Railroad—known for decades as the Standard Railroad of the World—had fallen on hard times. The railroad was no longer the economic

powerhouse it had been at the turn of the century, and it had allowed its physical plant to deteriorate. The railroad had let its prized symbol, Pennsylvania Station, fall into disrepair; the building was dirty inside and out and had a pathetic and ignominious air about it. After fifty years of service to the public, the station was doomed by the railroad's president, Jim Symes, who decided to raze the building and sell the real estate above the tracks. In 1963, despite public protest and pleas to preserve the great station, the railroad demolished it and erected in its place the new Madison Square Garden, deemed a visual monstrosity by most critics. Below the Garden, Amtrak, NJ Transit, and Long Island Rail Road trains still roll. But they serve an unimpressive facility not very different from an enlarged bus station.

The only good that came from Penn Station's demise were strict laws making similar crimes more difficult and a newly alert architectural preservation movement. As a result, later efforts to demolish Grand Central Terminal were thwarted. Presently there are plans to convert the United States Post Office, which stands across the street from the site of the old Pennsylvania Station and which was designed by the same firm, into a new railroad terminal over the former Pennsylvania Railroad tracks. This ambitious plan will give long-distance passengers a respectable entrance to New York.

CHAPTER 6

ADAPTIVE REUSE

As railroads change, once busy and prosperous depots are often left without trains to serve them. Sometimes an old station is simply too small to adequately handle a growing volume of traffic and is replaced by a larger station nearby. Sadly, in many cases, the passenger trains stop running and the station is abandoned. Either way, the railroad has to dispose of the disused railroad station. Stations may be left derelict and allowed to decay slowly into oblivion, unceremoniously demolished, converted to another function by the railroad, or sold. In the latter

PAGE 102: *Although passenger trains have not stopped at Rochelle, Illinois, for decades, the Burlington Northern Santa Fe still maintains the old passenger depot there and uses it for other purposes.* PAGE 103: *The Musée d'Orsay in Paris is one of the best-known adaptations of a railroad station in the Western world; it is now an art museum.* ABOVE: *Although twenty-five to thirty freight trains pass by this handsome limestone station every day, Waukesha, Wisconsin, is without passenger service. The old Soo Line Station, which hosted the famous Lake Cities passenger train until 1966, is now used by the Wisconsin Central as an office and maintenance depot.*

two situations, the old passenger station is often modified for a different use, limited only by the owner's imagination. With good fortune, the station's distinctive architecture is preserved and put to good use.

RAILROAD REUSE

The railroads have found many ways to utilize old passenger stations along their right-of-way, and many depots remain in place as operator stations long after passenger trains ceased to stop regularly. However, railroads in the United States and Canada today are largely controlled remotely from distant computerized dispatching centers, so few depots are still used that way on a regular basis.

Railroads will use old stations as on-line offices or as storage facilities and maintenance depots. Burlington Northern Santa Fe employs its old Chicago, Burlington & Quincy station in Rochelle, Illinois, for this latter purpose. A new railroad operator may find good use for an old train station. In the mid-1980s, the Southern Pacific sold several of its branch lines in Louisiana to a new short line called the Louisiana & Delta. This line decided to locate its offices in the traditional depot at New Iberia. This station is also a stop for Amtrak's triweekly Sunset Limited, although there is no longer a passenger agent there.

The Wisconsin Central Limited began freight operations over much of the former Soo Line in Wisconsin and Upper Michigan. (The new company took its name from the traditional Wisconsin Central that had operated portions of this route earlier in the century, but it is not related to this early company.) Wisconsin Central has used several on-line stations as offices, including those at Waukesha and Burlington, Wisconsin.

Conrail, the successor to several bankrupt northeastern railroads, is not known for its respectful treatment of traditional railroad structures. Yet, at several locations on its vast railroad network, it has continued to maintain a few old passenger stations. The classic stone

Richardsonian structure at East Brookfield, Massachusetts, is still used as a maintenance depot. Similarly, Conrail has reused the solid stone depots built for the Lake Shore & Michigan Southern at Ashtabula and Painesville, Ohio. Railroad stations in this sort of service are always in jeopardy of being demolished. If railroad maintenance needs are altered, or if an unsympathetic bean counter decides the old building has an excessive tax liability, the station may be reduced to rubble.

PRIVATE ADAPTATION

There are limitless nonrailroad applications for old train stations. One of most popular is the conversion of stations to station restaurants. All across the country there are depot diners. The former Housatonic Railroad (later part of the New Haven Railroad) station in Branchville, Connecticut, is now the Whistle Stop Bakery & Cafe. Inside, one can order one of several railroad-theme sandwiches, including an American Flyer.

In Cedar City, Utah, the old Union Pacific depot, which was built in 1923 to cater to tourist traffic for Zion National Park, now hosts a Godfather's Pizza restaurant and a gas station/convenience store. Passenger service was discontinued many years ago and now the tracks end several blocks from the station. In recent years, a motel complex has built up around the old station, giving the building an isolated appearance. However, the prominently displayed Union Pacific shield reveals the station's proper history. Pizza and railroad stations apparently make a good combination: many miles from Utah the former Boston & Maine Railroad station in Hardwick, Massachusetts, is now the Hardwick House of Pizza, which also serves grinders (the Yankee name for subs, hoagies, or heroes). Hardwick is a typical wooden station, but it has not served a passenger train in more than sixty years. A flood in the 1930s washed away the tracks, and afterward the Boston & Maine operated its trains over the nearby Boston & Albany's Ware River branch. Also, across town from the old Soo Line station in Waukesha, Wisconsin, is the old Chicago & North Western station, which is now an upscale restaurant called Louie's. Waukesha once had a third depot, but it was demolished to make way for a parking lot.

Many stations have found new life as museums, or as exhibits at museums. Some of these are internationally known, such as the grand Gare d'Orsay in Paris (see sidebar, pages 108–11), while most are relatively obscure, such as the Danbury Railway Museum in Danbury, Connecticut, or the small museum at the former Milwaukee Road depot in Whitewater, Wisconsin. The Comanche Crossing Historical Society in Strasburg, Colorado, maintains a collection of historic structures, including the Kansas Pacific's handsome wooden depot.

Often a train station is one of the most attractive buildings in town, so when the railroad wishes to dispose of their surplus structures, forward-thinking communities will make an effort to preserve the buildings. Connecticut was once crisscrossed by railroad lines; virtually every valley had at least one route. As a result, most towns had railroad service, and thus a railroad depot. Today, many of these depots still stand. A few host daily passenger trains, while others have been converted to alternative uses. Stafford Springs, once a popular resort, has a small but handsome brick depot downtown, which at one time served passenger trains for the New London Northern (later the Central Vermont Railway). Regular passenger service was discontinued shortly after World War II, but today it houses Stafford's Golden Age Club and the local historical society. In New Milford, Connecticut, the old railroad station has been beautifully restored and now serves as the chamber of commerce. Farther up the tracks, the Canaan Union Station, built in the 1890s to serve the Housatonic and the Central New England railroads (both later merged into the New Haven), now hosts the offices of a new railroad, which is also called the Housatonic, some shops, and a restaurant.

DESERT OASIS

Every desert needs its watering holes, and where the railroad crosses the desert, it builds its own oases. Much of the Nevada desert is rugged and

ABOVE: *A few miles south of Waukesha is Burlington, Wisconsin, the location of another former Soo Line station today in use as a railroad office. In recent years the restoration of rail service between Burlington and Chicago has been suggested, and someday this old station may again see regular passenger trains.*

mountainous, making railroad operations difficult. Caliente is an isolated desert community located along the Los Angeles and Salt Lake route of the Union Pacific in southeastern Nevada. The town sits at the lower end of Clover Creek Canyon, the natural low path that the railroad follows through this mountainous terrain. Caliente was once the railroad's desert oasis, with twenty-five hundred people employed by the Union Pacific. The town was division headquarters, a principal crew change point, the junction with a branch line, and the location of a freight-switching yard.

In 1923, to replace a station that had burned down, the Union Pacific built a large, Spanish Mission Revival–style building that functioned as a railroad station, a clubhouse, and a hotel for both its passengers and employees. It was designed by the famous Los Angeles architects John and Donald Parkinson, who later participated in the design of the Los Angeles Union Passenger Terminal. Caliente station is a classic example of the large Mission-style depots that once populated the Southwest. It contained fifty hotel rooms and two restaurants—a fine dining room and a railroader's beanery. The exterior is made of stucco and features rows of arches covering the outer walkway that faces the tracks. The interior is finished in fine oak. Without a doubt, this depot was, and is, the nicest building in town. When it was built in 1923, it cost more than $83,000.

The Union Pacific transferred its division headquarters to Las Vegas in 1948, and in the early 1970s it eliminated the Caliente crew change. The yard and branch line have been abandoned, although the main line through town is still very busy. Day and night, Union Pacific freight trains roll through town.

The Union Pacific leases the station to the town, which uses it as the chamber of commerce, a community center, and the town library. The depot is in beautiful condition and a few traditional baggage carts are displayed in front.

LIVINGSTON, MONTANA

One of the most attractive railroad stations in Big Sky Country is the former Northern Pacific station at Livingston, Montana. Situated east of Bozeman Pass, Livingston was a strategic railroad town—a principal division point where trains changed crews, the location of a large locomotive shop, and the site where helper locomotives were added to assist westbound trains climbing the steep Bozeman Pass grade.

ABOVE: *The Mission-Revival depot in Caliente, Nevada, once contained a hotel and two restaurants. Union Pacific no longer needs a station in Caliente, and the depot has been converted for non-railroad uses.* RIGHT: *Canaan Union Station, in Connecticut, was built to serve the Housatonic Railroad and the Central New England. Today the depot houses several offices and a restaurant.*

Livingston was also the Northern Pacific's gateway to Yellowstone National Park. A branch to the park met the main line here and, after the turn of the century, the Northern Pacific actively promoted the park as a vacation destination to attract riders to its trains. The railroad printed colorful brochures and arranged tours of the park and package vacations for travelers. In part through the efforts of the Northern Pacific, the image of Montana and Wyoming was transformed from that of a forbidding wasteland to an ideal vacation land.

As the choice destination of tourists and vacationers, Livingston needed a new depot, and in 1900 the railroad hired the St. Paul/Minneapolis firm of Reed & Stem, noted railroad station architects (who later worked on New York's Grand Central Terminal), to design a distinctive station. Working in the Italian Renaissance Revival–style, they combined three separate buildings with great curving canopies. The structures were built of sturdy red brick, faced with buff-colored brick and ornate terra cotta trim. The new depot opened in October 1902. For more than seven decades, it was a primary stop for Northern Pacific's flagship passenger train, the North Coast Limited.

Northern Pacific maintained passenger operations longer than many railroads in the United States. Throughout its nearly ninety-year existence, the Northern Pacific was never without a first-class passenger train. In 1970, the Northern Pacific merged with three other lines to form the Burlington Northern, the largest railroad in the United States at that time. A year later, the North Coast Limited was discontinued. For a few years, Amtrak served Livingston with the North Coast Hiawatha, but a round of draconian budget cuts killed this train in 1979, ending passenger service to Livingston.

Had shortsighted managers brought in the wrecking ball, the story of Northern Pacific's gateway to Yellowstone might have ended in a pile of unloved bricks, but fortunately this was not the case. Rather than destroying this fine station, Burlington Northern donated it to the town, and a local foundation restored the building at a cost of $800,000 (the original building cost $75,000). Today, the main building is the Western History Museum, which focuses on the crucial role of the Northern Pacific Railroad. Of the two smaller station buildings, one serves as the local chamber of commerce, while the other is a restaurant.

GARE D'ORSAY

Probably the most widely known adaptation of a railroad station is the conversion of the Gare d'Orsay in Paris to an art museum. This project received international attention from the media and is heralded as a splendid reuse of a historical structure. The Gare d'Orsay has been a sensation since its original opening in 1900 and has had great influence on the design of other railway stations in both Europe and the United States.

The Gare d'Orsay was the brainchild of the well-known Parisian architect Victor Laloux, a professor at the Ecole des Beaux-Arts. He had designed an earlier station at Tours, France, where he successfully employed the Beaux Arts architectural theory, which stresses a balanced design that fulfills its intended function. The Beaux Arts school had great influence on American architects, notably Henry Hobson Richardson, Kenneth Murchison, and Charles McKim. The Gare d'Orsay was Laloux's masterpiece, a model

BELOW AND OPPOSITE: *The Gare d'Orsay in Paris was built as a railroad station at the turn of the century and skillfully adapted in the 1980s to serve as an art museum. The station influenced the design of several stations around the world, including both great New York terminals—the old Pennsylvania Station and Grand Central Terminal. Today this great Parisian terminal is one of the city's premier museums.*

Les Schneider, Le Creusot

The Gare d'Orsay is one of the best known railroad station buildings in the world. Where passengers once boarded trains, museum patrons now come to gaze at great works.

design that proved enormously successful. It was constructed between 1897 and 1900, and its completion coincided with the Paris Exposition of 1900. Critics praised the station as one of the Exposition's prime attractions. Laloux perfectly melded Beaux Arts theory and classical architectural elements with the needs of a modern railway. The station was served exclusively by electrically powered trains, thus obviating the restrictions that steam, smoke, and coal dust had imposed on all previous railway station designs. Laloux dispensed with the traditional train shed by combining the waiting rooms, ticketing areas, and concourse into a single, large, open space. Rather than have a separate area for boarding, he brought the trains directly into the station via a network of tunnels that ran alongside the Seine River. Passengers reached the platforms directly from the waiting area by staircases. The station made prolific use of arches and columns and created a unique functional space. In his book *The Railroad Station*, Carroll Meeks describes the interior of the Gare d'Orsay as "a graceful vault with ample skylights," where "externally, enormous glazed archways signaled the entrances."

This station directly influenced the design of the Hamburg station in Germany, built between 1903 and 1906, and Copenhagen Central Station in Denmark, built between 1906 and 1911. It also inspired the design of the two great New York City stations, Pennsylvania Station and Grand Central Terminal. The influence of its Beaux Arts architectural layout and styling is evident in many smaller depots worldwide but particularly those in the United States built after 1900.

Despite its historic pre-eminence, the venerated Gare d'Orsay had fallen into disuse by the early 1960s. Its abandoned shell was used as a setting for Orson Welles' screen adaptation of Franz Kafka's *The Trial.* In the 1970s, the French president, Valéry Giscard d'Estaing, initiated the conversion of the station, and in the early 1980s it was reopened as the Musée du XIXᵉ Siècle (Museum of the Nineteenth Century), known colloquially as the Musée d'Orsay. Today it augments the Louvre, located across the Seine, and features a world-class display of nineteenth-century art.

The conversion of the Gare d'Orsay would have greatly pleased the Pennsylvania Railroad's Alexander Cassatt. Cassatt visited the station shortly after its opening and it inspired him to build New York's old Penn Station. Alexander's sister, Mary—one of the foremost American Impressionist artists—lived and worked as an expatriate in Paris.

OPPOSITE AND ABOVE: *It's no coincidence that the elegant former Northern Pacific station at Livingston, Montana, bears some architectural resemblance to New York's Grand Central Terminal: architects Reed & Stem worked on both stations. The Livingston station was built in 1902 and is still in use, albeit not as a railroad station.* PAGE 115–116: *Baltimore's Mt. Royal Station won an award for its skillful adaptation into an art school. A portion of the building is used as a library. Mt. Royal Station was designed by E. Francis Baldwin and Josias Pennington and built in 1894–1895 for the Baltimore & Ohio Railroad. Although it has not served a passenger train in many years, it is among the last American stations to retain its original train shed.*

BIBLIOGRAPHY

BOOKS

All Stations: A Journey Through 150 Years of Railway History. Paris, 1978

Alexander, Edwin P. *Down at the Depot: American Railroad Station from 1831 to 1920.* New York, 1970.

Barrett, Richard C. *Boston's Depots & Terminals.* Rochester, New York, 1996.

Biddle, Gordon. *Great Railway Stations of Britain.* Newton Abbot, 1986.

Binney, Marcus, and David Pearce. *Railway Architecture.* London, 1979.

Bradley, Bill. *The Last of the Great Stations.* Glendale, California, 1992.

Brittin, Robert P. *Central Vermont the South End: Remembering the "Banana Belt."* David City, Nebraska, 1995.

Burgess, George H., and Miles C. Kennedy. *Centennial History of the Pennsylvania Railroad.* Philadelphia, 1949.

Condit, Carl. *Port of New York, vols. 1 & 2.* Chicago, 1980, 1981.

Diehl, Lorraine B. *The Late Great Pennsylvania Station.* New York, 1985.

Droege, John A. *Passenger Terminals and Trains.* New York, 1916.

Fischler, Stan. *Next Stop Grand Central.* Ontario, 1986.

Grant, H. Roger, and Charles W. Bohi. *The Country Railroad Station in America.* Boulder, 1978.

Jackson, Alan A. *London's Termini.* Newton Abbot, 1969.

Lewis, Oscar. *The Big Four.* New York, 1938.

Marcigliano, John. *All Aboard for Union Station.* South Portland, Maine, 1991.

Marshall, David. *Grand Central.* New York, 1946.

Meeks, Carroll L.V. *The Railroad Station.* New Haven, Connecticut, 1956.

Middleton, William D. *Grand Central… the World's Greatest Railway Terminal.* San Marino, California, 1977.

— *Manhattan Gateway: New York's Pennsylvania Station.* Waukesha, Wisconsin, 1996.

Ochsner, Jeffery Karl. *H.H. Richardson Complete Architectural Works.* Cambridge, Massachusetts, 1984.

Potter, Janet Greenstein. *Great American Railroad Stations.* New York, 1996.

Richards, Jeffrey, and John M. MacKenzie. *The Railway Station: A Social History.* Oxford, 1986.

Scull, Theodore W. *Hoboken's Lackawanna Terminal.* New York, 1987.

Signor, John R. *Donner Pass: Southern Pacific's Sierra Crossing.* San Marino, California, 1985.

Signor, John R. *The Los Angeles and Salt Lake Railroad Company: Union Pacific's Historic Salt Lake Route.* San Marino, California, 1988.

Smith, Douglas N.W. *Canadian Rail Passenger Yearbook 1996-1997 Edition.* Ottawa, 1997.

Staufer, Alvin, and Bert Pennypacker. *Pennsy Power II.* 1968

Turner, Gregg M., and Melancthon W. Jacobus. *Connecticut Railroads…an Illustrated History.* Hartford, 1989.

Westing, Frederic. *Penn Station: Its Tunnels and Side Rodders.* Seattle, 1977.

PERIODICALS

Locomotive & Railway Preservation. Waukesha, Wisconsin.

The Official Guide of the Railways. New York.

Pacific RailNews. Waukesha, Wisconsin.

Trains. Waukesha, Wisconsin.

INDEX

Amtrak, 14, 31, 43, 46, 76, 78, 80, 85, 101, 104, 106
Architectural styles, 28
　　Art Deco, 55, 57
　　Art Nouveau, 72, *73*
　　Bauhaus, 55
　　Beaux Arts, 11, 43, 60, *61*, 61, 76, 99, 108, 110
　　Colonial Revival, 28
　　Federalist, 28
　　Gothic Revival, 28, 81, 85
　　Greek Revival, 98
　　neoclassical, 43, 57, 76
　　Norman Revival, 64, *65*
　　Queen Anne, 28, *29*, 29
　　Renaissance Revival, 78, 106
　　Romanesque, 28, 43, 80, 89
　　Spanish Mission, 28, *30*, 31, 59, *59*, *78*, *79*, 106
　　Tudor, 28
　　Victorian, 43, 57, 81, 85, *85*, 99
Austria
　　Karlsplatz (Vienna), 14, *15*
Baldwin, E. Francis, 28, 113
Baltimore & Ohio Railroad, 28, 29, 32, 33
Barlow, William Henry, 51, 81
Beard, A. Len, 37
Belgium, 58
　　Antwerp, 22, *22*, 72, *73*
Brussels, 58
Boston & Albany Railroad, 31, 45, 105
Boston & Maine Railroad, 28, 105
British Rail, 71
Broad Street Station (London), 57
Broad Street Station (Philadelphia), 54, 98, 99
Burlington Northern Railroad, 106
Burlington Northern Santa Fe Railroad, 104
Burlington Railroad, 43
Burnham, Daniel, 43
Bush, Lincoln, 60

Calatrava, Santiago, 14
California
　　Oakland, 54
　　San Francisco, 58, 59, *59*
　　Santa Fe Station (Barstow), *30*, 31
　　Southern Pacific Station (Sacramento), 78, *78*, 79
　　Union Passenger Terminal (Los Angeles), 57, 106
　　Union Station (San Diego), 79, *79*, 80
Cameron, Edward B., 64
Canada, 14
　　Montreal, 37, 54, 57, 58
　　Toronto, 58
Canadian Pacific Windsor Station (Montreal), 54, *55*
Cassatt, Alexander, 99, 101, 111
Central New England Railroad, 105
Central Pacific Railroad, 78, 79
Central Station (Antwerp), 22, *22*
Central Station (Helsinki), 82, *83*
Central Vermont Railroad, 45, 76, 80, 93, 105
Central Vermont Station (Shelburne), *74*, 76
Charing Cross Station (London), 62, *63*
Chicago, Burlington & Quincy Railroad, 104
Chicago & Alton Railroad, 43
Chicago & North Western Railroad, 31, 36, 37, 54, 105
Cobb, Henry Ives, 36
Cologne Station (Germany), *49*, 51, *51*, 54
Colorado, 36
　　Denver, *42*, 43
　　Strasburg, 105
Connecticut
　　Branchville, 105
　　Canaan, *86–87*, 89, 105, 106, *107*
　　Hartford, 80, *81*, *84*, 85
　　Wallingford, 80
　　Windsor, 80, 85, *85*
Conrail, 104, 105

Cooper, Peter, 33
Coutan, Jules, 11
Crocker, Charlie, 79.
CSX Transportation, 33
Cumbres & Toltec Scenic Railroad, 36

Delaware, Lackawanna & Western Railroad, 54, 60
　　Phoebe Snow, 60–61
Denmark
　　Copenhagen, 58, 111
Denver, Rio Grande & Western Railroad, 31, 36

Edison, Thomas, 61
Erie-Lackawanna Railroad, 61
Euston Street Station (London), 57, 98, 99
Finland
　　Helsinki, 82
Fox, Charles, 98
Fox River Valley Railroad, 36
France
　　Gare de Lyon (Paris), *20*, 21, *48*, 51
　　Gare d'Orsay (Paris), 108, *108*, 109, *109*, 110, *110*, *111*
　　Gare du Nord (Paris), 66, *66*
　　Lyons, *24*, 25, *25*
　　Nice, 89, *89*
　　Part Dieu (Lyons), *13*, 14
　　Très Grande Vitesse Railroad, 14
Frost, Charles S., 28, 31, 36–37
Furness, Frank, 99

Gare Centrale Station (Montreal), 57, 58
Gare de Lyon (Paris), *20*, 21, *48*, 51
Gare d'Orsay (Paris), 108, *108*, 109, *109*, 110, *110*, *111*
Gare du Nord (Paris), 66, *66*
Germany, 58
　　Berlin, 58
　　Cologne, *49*, 51, *51*, 54, 58
　　Frankfort, 14, 22, *23*, 66, *66*
　　Hamburg, 58, 111
　　Koblenz Station, 62, *62*

Grand Central Station (New York City)
8, *9*, *10*, 11, 51, 55, 101
Granger, Alfred Hoyt, 28, 36
Great Northern Pacific Railroad, 37
Green Mountain Railroad, 76
Gulf, Mobile & Ohio Railroad, 40, 43

Hardwick, Philip, 98
Harvey House Restaurants, 31, 80
Hill, James J., 37
Housatonic Railroad, 85, 105
Hudson Line, 8, 55, 99
Hughitt, Marvin, 36
Hunt, Jarvis, 40, 43
Huntingdon & Broad Top Railroad, 93

Illinois
Chicago, 28, *28*, 36, *38*, 40, 43,
45, 46, *46*, *47*
Joliet, 40, *41*, 43
Rochelle, *102*, 104
Illinois Central Railroad, 43
Italy
Milan, *12*, 14, 21, *21*, 55

Japan, 58
Mishima Station, 64, *64*
Osaka, 58
Shimobe, 71, *71*
Shin-Juku (Tokyo), *18–19*, 21
Tokyo, 58
Japanese National Railway, 58

Kansas Pacific Railroad, 105
Karlsplatz Station (Vienna), 14, *15*
Keller, George, 80
Koblenz Station (Germany), 62, *62*
Kuala Lumpur Station (Malaysia), *50*,
51

Lake Shore & Michigan Southern
Railroad, 105
Laloux, Victor, 108, 110
La Salle Street Station (Chicago), 43
Link, Theodore C., 64
Liverpool Street Station (London), 57,
70, 71

London & Birmingham Railway, 98
Long Island Railroad, 101
Louisiana & Delta Railroad, 104
Louisville & Nashville Railroad, 89

MacQuarrie, John A., 78, 79
Malaysia, *50*, 51
Maryland
Ellicott City, 32, *32*, 33, *33*
Laurel, *26*, 28
Mt. Royal, 28, 113, *114–115*
Oakland Station, 29, *29*, 31
Pennsylvania Station (Baltimore),
94, 95
Point of Rocks, 95, *95*
Massachusetts
Amherst, 93, *93*
Boston, 11
East Brookfield, 105
Hardwick, 105
North Station (Boston), 55
Palmer, *44*, 45
Park Square Station (Boston), 54
McKim, Charles, 99, 101, 108
Metro North Railroad, 11
Midland Railway, 81
Milwaukee Road, 36, 37, 43, 45, 105
Hiawatha service, 14, 37
Minnesota
Minneapolis, 36, 37, *37*
St. Paul, 36, 37
Mishima Station (Japan), 64, *64*
Missouri
St. Louis, *39*, 40, 64, *65*, 72, *72*
Missouri Pacific Railroad, 40
Montfort, Richard, 89
Murchison, Kenneth, 60, 61, 76, 78,
108

National Register of Historic Places,
33
Netherlands, 58
Amsterdam, 14, 58
Breda, 14, *68—69*, 71
Eindhoven, 14
Rotterdam, 58

New Hampshire
Woodsville, 27, 28
New Haven Railroad, 11, 85, 105
New Jersey
Hoboken, 54, 58, 60, *60*, 61, *61*,
76
New London Northern Railroad, 45,
80, 93, 105
New Mexico, 36
Chama, *34–35*, 36
New York
Buffalo, 55, 60
Grand Central Station, 8, *9*, *10*,
11, 51, 55, 101
New York, New Haven & Hartford
Railroad, 55
New York Central Railroad, 11, 40,
55, 99
New York & Harlem Railroad, 55
Norcross, Orland, 80
Northern Central Railroad, 76
Northern Pacific Railroad, 106, 113
North Station (Boston), 55
North Western Passenger Station
(Chicago), 28, *28*, 54

Ohio
Ashtabula, 105
Cleveland, 43
Painesville, 105
Union Terminal (Cincinnati), 55,
57
Omaha Railway, 37

Park Square Station (Boston), 54
Part Dieu Station (Lyons), *13*, 14
Pennington, Josias, 113
Pennsylvania, 28
Huntingdon, *90–91*, 93
Philadelphia, 43, 54
Scranton, 76
Pennsylvania Railroad, 40, 43, 54, 57,
58, 78, 93, 99, 101
Pennsylvania Station (Baltimore), 76,
77, 78, *94*, 95
Pennsylvania Station (New York City),
61, 78, 99, *100*, 101, *101*

Pittsburgh, Fort Wayne & Chicago Railroad, 43

Railroads
    Amtrak, 14
    Baltimore & Ohio, 28, 29, 32, 33
    Boston & Albany, 31, 45, 105
    Boston & Maine, 28, 105
    British Rail, 71
    Burlington, 43
    Burlington Northern, 106
    Burlington Northern Santa Fe, 104
    Canadian, 14
    Canadian Pacific, 54
    Central New England, 105
    Central Pacific, 78, 79
    Central Vermont, 45, 76, 80, 93, 105
    Chicago, Burlington & Quincy, 104
    Chicago & Alton, 43
    Chicago & North Western, 31, 36, 37, 54, 105
    commuter, 8, 11, 14, 46, 58, 61, 78, 80, 95
    corridor, 14
    Cumbres & Toltec Scenic, 36
    decline in, 14, 33
    Delaware, Lackawanna & Western, 54, 60
    Denver, Rio Grande & Western, 31, 36
    early, 12, 14
    Erie-Lackawanna, 61
    Eurostar, 56, 57
    Fox River Valley, 36
    Great Northern Pacific, 37
    Green Mountain Railroad, 76
    Gulf, Mobile & Ohio, 40, 43
    Housatonic, 85, 105
    Hudson Line, 8, 55, 99
    Huntingdon & Broad Top, 93
    Illinois Central, 43
    interurban, 43
    Japanese National Railway, 58
    Kansas Pacific, 105

Lake Shore & Michigan Southern, 105
London & Birmingham Railway, 98
Long Island, 101
Louisiana & Delta, 104
Louisville & Nashville, 89
Metro North, 11
Midland Railway, 81
Milwaukee Road, 14, 36, 37, 43, 45
Missouri Pacific, 40
narrow-gauge, 36, 43
New Haven, 11, 85, 105
New London Northern, 45, 80, 93, 105
New York, New Haven & Hartford, 55
New York Central, 11, 40, 55, 99
New York & Harlem, 55
Northern Central, 76
Northern Pacific, 106, 113
Omaha Railway, 37
Pennsylvania, 40, 43, 54, 57, 58, 76, 78, 93, 99, 101
Pittsburgh, Fort Wayne & Chicago, 43
Rio Grande, 42, 43
Rock Island, 43
Rutland, Boston & Main, 76
Santa Fe, 43, 57, 79, 80
Southern Pacific, 57, 58, 78, 104
Tennessee Central, 89
Très Grande Vitesse, 14, 24, 25, 25
Union Pacific, 57, 79, 105, 106
Western Maryland, 76
Western Pacific, 79
Wisconsin Central, 104
Raynaud, Léonce, 66
Reading Terminal (Philadelphia), 54
Richardson, Henry Hobson, 31, 45, 80, 85, 108
Rio Grande Railroad
    California Zephyr, 43
    Ski Train, 42, 43
Rock Island Railroad, 43

Rocky Mountain Rocket, 43
Rutland, Boston & Main Railroad, 76

Saarinen, Eliel, 82
St. Pancras Station (London), 51, 52–53, 54, 57, 81, 82, 82
Sanders, J. David, 37
Santa Fe Railroad, 43, 57, 79, 80
Scott, Giles Gilbert, 81, 82
Shin-Juku Station (Tokyo), 18–19, 21
South Dakota, 37
Southern Pacific Railroad, 57, 58, 78, 104
Southern Pacific Station (Sacramento), 78, 78, 79
South Station (Boston), 11
Spain
    Madrid, 58, 62, 62
Stanford, Leland, 78, 79
Stations
    adaptations, 102–115
    Antwerp (Belgium), 22, 22
    Broad Street Station (London), 57
    Broad Street Station (Philadelphia), 54, 98, 99
    Canadian Pacific Windsor Station (Montreal), 54, 55
    Central Station (Helsinki), 82, 83
    Charing Cross Station (London), 62, 63
    Chicago & North Western Terminal (Chicago), 31, 36, 37, 54
    classic, 74–95
    Cologne (Germany), 49, 51, 51
    Cologne Station (Germany), 54
    early, 26, 28, 31, 32, 33, 36, 37
    Euston Street Station (London), 57, 98, 99
    Frankfort (Germany), 22, 23, 66, 66
    Gare Centrale Station (Montreal), 57, 58
    Gare de Lyon (Paris), 20, 21, 48, 51
    Gare d'Orsay (Paris), 108, 108, 109, 109, 110, 110, 111

Gare du Nord (Paris), 66, *66*
Grand Central Station (New York City), 8, *9*, *10*, 11, 51, 55, 101
Hoboken (New Jersey), 54, 58, 60, *60*, 61, *61*
Karlsplatz (Vienna), 14, *15*
Koblenz Station (Germany), 62, *62*
La Salle Street Station (Chicago), 43
Liverpool Street Station (London), *57*, *70*, 71
Lyons (France), *24*, 25, *25*
Milan (Italy), *12*, 14, 21, *21*, 55
North Station (Boston), 55
Oakland (Maryland), 29, *29*, 31
Park Square Station (Boston), 54
Part Dieu (Lyons), *13*, 14
Pennsylvania Station (Baltimore), 76, *77*, 78, *94*, 95
Pennsylvania Station (New York City), 61, 78, 99, *100*, 101, *101*
Reading Terminal (Philadelphia), 54
St. Pancras Station (London), 51, *52–53*, 54, 57, 81, 82, *82*
Shin-Juku (Tokyo), *18–19*, 21
Southern Pacific Station (Sacramento), 78, *78*, 79
South Station (Boston), 11
stub-end, 57, 58, 72
styles, 11, 28
Thirtieth Street Station (Philadelphia), 43, 57, 99
through, 57, 58
Union Passenger Terminal (Los Angeles), 57, 106
Union Station (Canaan), *86–87*, 89, 105, 106, *107*
Union Station (Chicago), *38*, 40, 43, 45, 46, *46*, 47
Union Station (Cleveland), 43
Union Station (Denver), *42*, 43
Union Station (Joliet), 40, *41*, 43
Union Station (Kansas City), 43
Union Station (Nashville), *88*, 89
Union Station (New London), 80, *80*

Union Station (Palmer), *44*, 45
Union Station (St. Louis), *39*, 40, 64, *65*, 72, *72*
Union Station (San Diego), 79, *79*, 80
Union Station (Toronto), 58
Union Terminal (Cincinnati), 55, 57
Victoria Station (London), *17–18*, 18
Waterloo Station (London), 54, *54*, *56*, 57
Western Pacific Terminal (Oakland), 54
Stephenson, George, 12, 98
Stephenson, Robert, 98
Sweden
  Stockholm, 58
Switzerland
  Geneva, 14
  Zurich, 14
Symes, James, 99, 101

Tennessee
  Nashville, *88*, 89
Tennessee Central Railroad, 89
Terminals. *See* Stations
Thirtieth Street Station (Philadelphia), 43, 57, 99
Toudoire, Marius, 21, 51
Train sheds, *51*, 54, 55, *70*, 71, 72, *72*
  arched, 51, *51*, 54, *54*, 66, *66*
  balloon, 51, 54, 72, *73*, 82
  Bush, 54, 60, 78
  iron, 51
  single-span, 54
  truss-type, 66, *66*

Union Pacific Railroad, 57, 79, 105, 106
Union Passenger Terminal (Los Angeles), 57, 106
Union Station
  Canaan (Connecticut), *86–87*, 89, 105, 106, 107
  Chicago (Illinois), *38*, 40, 43, 45, 46, *46*, 47

Cincinnati (Ohio), 55, 57
Cleveland (Ohio), 43
Denver (Colorado), *42*, 43
Joliet (Illinois), 40, *41*, 43
Kansas City (Kansas), 43
Nashville (Tennessee), *88*, 89
New London (Connecticut), 80, *80*
St. Louis (Missouri), *39*, 40, 64, *65*, 72, *72*
San Diego (California), 79, *79*, 80
Toronto (Canada), 58
United Kingdom, 58
  London, *17–18*, 18, 54, *54*, 57
  York, 66, 67
Utah, 36
  Cedar City, 105
  Thompson, 31, *31*
Vanderbilt, Cornelius, 51, 55
Vermont
  Bellows Falls, 76
  Central Vermont Railway Station (Shelburne), *74*, 76
  Chester, 76
  Ludlow, 76
Victoria Station (London), *16–17*, 17

Wagner, Otto, 14
Waterloo Station (London), 54, *54*, 56, 57
Weinman, Adolph A., 101
Western Maryland Railroad, 76
Western Pacific Railroad, 79
Western Pacific Terminal (Oakland), 54
Wilson, Francis W., 31
Wisconsin
  Beloit, 36
  Burlington, 105, *105*
  Green Bay, 36
  Madison, 36, 37
  Oshkosh, 36
  Watertown, 36, *36*
  Waukesha, 105
  Wausau, 36
Wisconsin Central Railroad, 104